UNDERSTANDING DOCTRINE

UNDERSTANDING DOCTRINE

Its Relevance and Purpose for Today

Alister McGrath

Hodder & Stoughton
LONDON SYDNEY AUCKLAND TORONTO

The author and publisher are grateful to Collins Publications for permission to quote from the following published works of C.S. Lewis: *Surprised by Joy*; *Till We Have Faces*; *Screwtape Proposes a Toast*; *Christian Reflections*.

Biblical quotations are taken from the New International Version.

British Library Cataloguing in Publication Data
McGrath, Alister E. (Alister Edgar) *1953–*
    Understanding doctrine.
    1. Christian doctrine
    I. Title
    230

ISBN 0-340-53822-8

Published by Hodder and Stoughton, a division of Hodder and Stoughton Ltd, Mill Road, Dunton Green, Sevenoaks, Kent TN13 2YA. Editorial Office: 47 Bedford Square, London WC1B 3DP

Typeset by Hewer Text Composition Services, Edinburgh
Printed in Great Britain by Clays Ltd, St. Ives plc

Contents

Introduction   vii
1 Getting Started   1

Part I   Doctrine: What it is   9
2 The Way Things Are: Doctrine and Description   11
3 Responding to God: Doctrine and Revelation   22
4 Intellect and Feelings: Doctrine and Experience   39
5 Believing and Belonging: Doctrine and
    Christian Identity   53

Part II   Doctrine: Why it matters   71
6 Doctrine and Faith   73
7 Doctrine and the Christian Life   84
8 Is Christianity Possible without Doctrine?   99
9 The Coherence of Doctrine and the Challenge
    of Heresy   112
10 Wrestling with Doctrine: Discovering the Creeds   121

Part III   Some Key Doctrines Examined   133
11 The Person of Jesus Christ   135
12 The Work of Jesus Christ   150
13 The Trinity   167

Conclusion   177

Bibliography   179

INTRODUCTION

Doctrine! The very word sends shivers down a lot of spines. The mental journey between 'doctrine' and 'doctrinaire' is all too short and easy for comfort. Doctrine suggests something petty and pedantic. It conjures up images of hard-bitten theologians, scrabbling furiously and pointlessly over words. It even evokes painful memories of the Spanish Inquisition, when men and women suffered for not accepting the right ideas. Doctrine seems like a relic of a bygone age. It may have been important once upon a time. But not now. There is a widespread feeling that doctrine is an irrelevance to modern Christian faith and Christian life. One influential Christian writer once remarked that some of the works he read on Christian doctrine made as much sense and were just about as exciting as mathematical tables!

This attitude is perfectly understandable. Many people who have had a profound experience of God find that doctrines seem somehow terribly *unreal*. Take a woman who has felt herself overwhelmed by the closeness of God at the birth of her first child. Or a student who experiences an awesome sense of God's forgiveness as she prays. Or someone who, like the present writer, has been out alone in the Arabian desert in the depths of the night, and caught a sense of the immensity of God amidst the splendour of the starry heavens. All these have felt the presence of God. And if they turn from this experience to consider Christian doctrines, they often feel a sense of anticlimax. The doctrines seem stale and frigid in comparison with what they know of

God. They just don't measure up to the real thing. They seem like mathematical equations, cold and impersonal. Surely God's not like that! What conceivable relevance can they have? Why bother with them? Surely doctrine has no relevance for the ordinary believer.

Now that I've sketched the problems people have with doctrine, I suppose you expect me to say something like this: 'Well, you're wrong! Doctrine is vitally important, and you ought to accept this as a fact, and stop complaining.' However, I want to say nothing of the sort. You are right. I feel exactly the same way myself. Doctrine *does* seem something of an irrelevance. It does seem more than a little pedantic. And it does seem strange to be concerned with precise neat little formulas about God. All these are real, not imagined, problems. *Christianity is not, and never has been, about finding the right combination of words! It is about encountering the living and loving God.*

But there is more to doctrine than you might think. And, curiously, doctrine actually deals with exactly the same problems just noted. If we want to talk about God, to share our experiences of him, or to try and explain why Jesus Christ is so important, we end up making doctrinal statements. Without fully realising it, every Christian believer is concerned with doctrine. In this book, I want to try to explore what doctrine is, and why it matters. Thinking about doctrine is actually an excellent way of deepening our understanding of our faith. And it is certainly not an irrelevance! But that is to skip ahead to the conclusion of this book. Let's begin somewhere more suitable.

1 GETTING STARTED

Commitment is fundamental to any but the most superficial forms of human existence. In his famous essay 'The Will to Believe', the celebrated psychologist William James makes it clear that there are some choices in life which cannot be avoided. To be human is to make decisions. We are all obliged to choose between options which are, in James' words, 'living, forced and momentous'. In matters of morality, politics and religion, we must make conscious choices – and, as James stresses, our whole life hangs upon the choice made.

Every movement which has ever competed for the loyalty of human beings has done so on the basis of a set of beliefs. Whether the movement is religious or political, philosophical or artistic, the same pattern emerges – a group of ideas, of beliefs, are affirmed to be, in the first place, true, and in the second, important. It is impossible to live life to its fullness, and avoid encountering claims for our loyalty of one kind or another. Marxism, socialism, atheism – all alike demand that we consider their claims. The same is true of liberalism, whether in its religious or political forms. As Alasdair MacIntyre demonstrated so persuasively in his *Whose Justice? Which Rationality?*, liberalism is committed to a definite set of beliefs, and hence to certain values. It is one of the many virtues of MacIntyre's important work that it mounts a devastating critique of the idea that liberalism represents some kind of privileged and neutral vantage point from which other doctrinal or religious traditions (such as evangelicalism) may be evaluated. Rather, liberalism entails precommitment to liberal beliefs and values. Liberal beliefs (and thus values) affect liberal decisions – in ethics, religion and politics.

Time and time again, life-changing decisions are demanded of us. How shall I vote at the next election? What do I think about the riddle of human destiny? What form of educational system do I consider to be best? Is the use of deadly force justifiable to defend democracy? What rights do animals have? All these questions force us to think about our beliefs – and make a choice. You cannot sit on the fence throughout life, as William James demonstrated with such remarkable clarity. To suspend judgement on every question which life raises is to be trapped in an insipid agnosticism, where all the great questions arising out of human experience receive the same shallow response: 'I don't know – and I don't care.'

Thinking people need to construct and inhabit mental worlds. They need to be able to discern some degree of ordering within their experience, to make sense of its riddles and enigmas. They need to be able to structure human existence in the world, to allow it to possess meaning and purpose, and to allow decisions to be made concerning the future of that existence. In order for anyone – Christian, atheist, Marxist or Moslem – to make informed moral decisions, it is necessary to have a set of values concerning human life. Those values are determined by beliefs, and those beliefs are stated as doctrines. Christian doctrine thus provides a fundamental framework for Christian living.

Christianity is not a set of woolly and ill-defined (but vaguely benevolent) attitudes to the world in general and other human beings in particular. It is not an unstructured assortment of emotions or feelings. Rather, it centres on beliefs about Jesus Christ, which give rise to specific religious and moral attitudes to God, other human beings, and the world. Jesus Christ is the beginning, the centre and the end of the Christian message of hope. At the heart of the Christian faith stands a person, not a doctrine – but a person who gives rise to doctrine the moment we begin to wrestle with the question, 'Who is Jesus Christ?' The idea that we can somehow worship, adore or imitate Jesus Christ without developing doctrines about him is indefensible.

The novelist Dorothy L. Sayers is perhaps best known as the creator of Lord Peter Wimsey, a distinguished aristocratic amateur detective. She was also no mean amateur theologian, who was thoroughly impatient with those who declared that doctrine was 'hopelessly irrelevant' to the life and thought of the ordinary Christian believer. 'Ministers of the Christian religion often assert that it is, present it for consideration as though it were, and, in fact, by their faulty exposition of it make it so.' She was especially – and rightly – scornful of those who argue that it is principles, not doctrines, which distinguish Christianity from paganism. Writing in the depths of the Second World War, she declared:

> That you cannot have Christian principles without Christ is becoming increasingly clear, because their validity depends upon Christ's authority; and, as we have seen, the totalitarian states, having ceased to believe in Christ's authority, are logically quite justified in repudiating Christian principles. If 'the average man' is required to 'believe in Christ' and accept his authority for 'Christian principles', it is surely relevant to inquire who or what Christ is, and why his authority should be accepted . . . It is quite useless to say that it doesn't matter particularly who or what Christ was or by what authority he did those things, and that even if he was only a man, he was a very nice man and we ought to live by his principles: for that is merely Humanism, and if the 'average man' in Germany chooses to think that Hitler is a nicer sort of man with still more attractive principles, the Christian Humanist has no answer to make.

Why do Christians take the teachings of Jesus Christ so seriously? Why do they attribute such authority to him?

Underlying the authority of Jesus is the Christian understanding of who he is. Christians regard Christ as authoritative because, in the end, they recognise him to be none other than God himself, coming among us as one of us. The authority of Jesus Christ rests in his being God incarnate. His teaching is lent dignity, weight and authority by his identity. And that identity can only be spelled out fully by the doctrine of the person of Christ. Christian principles thus rest on Christian doctrine.

Some writers have suggested that the authority of Christ rests upon the excellence of his moral and religious teaching. This position initially sounds attractive; on closer inspection, however, it turns out actually to undermine that very authority. By what standards do we judge his teaching? The argument rests on knowing in advance what moral or religious teachings are to be regarded as outstanding. Jesus Christ is then regarded as authoritative, to the extent that he echoes these already existing standards. He is judged by a higher authority – what these writers regard as morally and religiously acceptable. For classical Christian thought, it is existing human religious and moral ideas which are to be challenged and judged by Jesus Christ; for these modern writers, it is existing notions of morality and religion which are to judge Jesus Christ. Christ is thus placed firmly under human authority, denied any role of challenging and overturning accepted human ideas and values.

It may seem very attractive to see Jesus as some sort of projection or validation of our own standards and aspirations. Yet if we allow that Jesus has authority simply because he echoes what we happen to believe to be right, we are setting ourselves above him in judgement. It is our own concepts of morality, our own standards (wherever they come from) that are judging him. And all too often those standards are little more than the prejudices of our own culture. By judging Jesus in this way, we lock ourselves into our own situation. We are prisoners of our culture, unable to see its limitations. We are unwilling to accept criticism from outside it. If Jesus echoes our own values and aspirations, we gladly accept his support; if Jesus should happen to challenge them, we dismiss him, or choose to ignore the challenge. Jesus is thus denied any possibility of transforming us, by challenging our presuppositions. We are reluctant to hear him, where he does not echo our own voices. If Jesus has any authority in this way, it is simply as a passive echo of our own ideas and values. 'I happen to buy most of what Jesus said, but not because it's in the Bible or because he said it, but rather because I find it existentially valid. And I have to be candid enough to say that there are a few things Jesus said that I can't buy' (Thomas Maurer).

It is for this reason that doctrine is of central importance. Christianity does not assert that Christ has authority on account of the excellence or acceptability of his teaching; rather, the teaching of Christ has authority and validity on account of who he is – God incarnate. The New Testament provides ample justification of this point; throughout his writings, Paul begins by making doctrinal affirmations, and then proceeds to draw moral conclusions. Doctrine comes first; moral and religious principles follow. For example, the doctrine of the resurrection leads to an attitude of hope in the face of adversity; the doctrine of the incarnation of Christ leads to an attitude of humility on the part of believers; the doctrine of the reconciliation of believers to God through Christ leads to a plea that believers should be reconciled among themselves.

Doctrine about Christ arises from the need to tell the truth about Christ; to explain who he is, and his significance for the human situation. To fail to develop doctrines about Jesus Christ is to reveal a dangerously shallow commitment to him, and to the unremitting human quest for truth. Doctrine reflects a commitment to truth on the one hand, and to the centrality of Jesus Christ to the Christian faith on the other. It is no good to mumble vague generalities about Jesus being 'the moral educator of mankind' or 'a good man who deserves to be imitated'. It is necessary to spell out, as precisely as possible, what it is that Christians have found, and continue to find, so profoundly attractive, authoritative and challenging about him.

Doctrine is the Christian church giving an account of itself, as it answers to the call of God in Jesus Christ. It is the response of the human mind to God, as love is the response of the human heart. The nucleus of the Christian faith is the mystery of the person of Jesus Christ. What do his crucifixion and resurrection tell us about ourselves? about God? about the world? In what way can they change our situation? What must we do if we are to appropriate, to make our own, the new possibilities and opportunities opened up by this most dramatic manifestation of the power of God at work in human history?

If doctrine at times seems to be little more than a barren repetition of ancient words and formulas, approaching a mindless ritual, it is because we have failed to appreciate its vitality and relevance. The failure of human language to capture the richness of experience has long been known and lamented. The Austrian philosopher Ludwig Wittgenstein pointed out that it was impossible to describe the aroma of coffee using words; imagine how much worse it must be when trying to describe something as profound as the Christian experience of being redeemed from sin. Doctrine is an attempt to spell out in human words something which cannot really be expressed in words. Hilary of Poitiers, one of the more perceptive Christian writers of the fourth century, captured this dilemma perfectly: 'We are compelled to attempt what is unattainable, to climb where we cannot reach, to speak what we cannot utter. Instead of the bare adoration of faith, we are compelled to entrust the profound matters of faith to the perils of human language.' Doctrine may seem to be excessively preoccupied with the details of verbal formulas – but this reflects the basic Christian conviction that, if the truth about Jesus Christ is proclaimed and accepted, the human situation can be transformed. Doctrine aims to provide a springboard to propel us into a personal response to the truth and the love of God, revealed in Jesus Christ. 'To know Christ is to know his benefits,' as the sixteenth-century theologian Philip Melanchthon wrote. Properly understood, doctrine may be continually rediscovered as something newly meaningful for our own day and age.

In practice, most Christians probably do not need to be persuaded that doctrine is important. Most realise the importance of doctrine to their faith, and some may have found the arguments presented in this chapter unnecessary. In his comedy *Le Bourgeois Gentilhomme*, the seventeenth-century French playwright Molière tells of the astonishment of Monsieur Jourdain on being told that, when he asked for his slippers and nightcap, he was speaking prose. 'Good Lord!', he exclaimed. 'I have been speaking prose for more than forty years without knowing it.' In much the same way, most Christians make doctrinal statements without realising it. Every time a hymn is sung, the creed is recited, sermons are heard, or a scriptural passage is discussed – matters of doctrine are involved.

Nevertheless, many Christians do have difficulty with doctrine. They may be puzzled over why it should have caused so much controversy. They may occasionally have wondered if it might be possible to abandon doctrine, without doing any real harm to the Christian faith. And for some, certain doctrines cause considerable bewilderment – such as that most mysterious of all doctrines, the Trinity. The remainder of this book aims to deal with those questions. We begin by considering in more detail precisely what doctrine is.

Part I

Doctrine: What it is

Christian doctrine is the response of the Christian church to God, as he has revealed himself, especially in Scripture and through Jesus Christ. It is an obedient, responsible and faithful attempt to make sense of the cluster of astonishing and exciting possibilities opened up by the coming of Jesus Christ. As the following chapters will make clear, doctrine is a complicated matter, which is not adequately described simply as 'Christian teachings'. Doctrine serves four major purposes. It aims:

1. to tell the truth about the way things are.
2. to respond to the self-revelation of God.
3. to address, interpret and transform human experience.
4. to give Christians, as individuals and as a community, a sense of identity and purpose.

We shall explore each of these aspects of the nature of doctrine in the chapters which follow.

2   THE WAY THINGS ARE: DOCTRINE AND DESCRIPTION

'Relevance' and 'meaningfulness' were words which captured the imagination of a recent generation. Unless something was 'relevant' or 'meaningful', there was no point in bothering with it. Christian doctrine, many suggested, was outdated and irrelevant. The brave new world that was dawning could manage very well without such relics of the past.

The danger of all this is clear. Beneath all the rhetoric about relevance lies a profoundly disturbing possibility – that people may base their lives upon an illusion, upon a blatant lie. The attractiveness of a belief is all too often inversely proportional to its truth. In the sixteenth century, the radical writer and preacher Thomas Müntzer led a revolt of German peasants against their political masters. On the morning of the decisive encounter between the peasants and the armies of the German princes, Müntzer promised that those who followed him would be unscathed by the weapons of their enemies. Encouraged by this attractive and meaningful belief, the peasants stiffened their resolve.

The outcome was a catastrophe. Six thousand peasants were slaughtered in the ensuing battle, and six hundred captured. Barely a handful escaped. Their belief in invulnerability was relevant. It was attractive. It was meaningful. It was also a crude and cruel lie, without any foundation in truth. The last hours of that pathetic group of trusting men rested on an utter illusion. It was only when the first salvoes cut some of their number to ribbons that they realised that they had been deceived.

To allow 'relevance' to be given greater weight than truth is a mark of intellectual shallowness and moral irresponsibility. The first, and most fundamental, of all questions must be: is it true? is this worthy of belief and trust? Once this has been established, the relevance of the belief in question may be considered. It is quite possible that most readers will find the contents of the *Annual Yearbook of Statistics* for 1965 utterly tedious – yet they may rest assured that those contents are reliable. They chronicle the way things were. They are a record of facts. Truth is certainly no guarantee of relevance – but no-one can build their personal life around a lie.

Christian doctrine aims to describe the way things are. It is concerned to tell the truth, in order that we may enter into and act upon that truth. It is an expression of a responsible and caring faith – a faith which is prepared to give an account of itself, and give careful consideration to its implications for the way in which we live. To care about doctrine is to care about the reliability of the foundations of the Christian life. It is to be passionately concerned that our actions and attitudes, our hopes and our fears, are a response to *God* – and not something or someone making claims to divinity, which collapse upon closer inspection.

Perhaps the German church struggle of the 1930s highlights the importance of doctrine in the modern world. When Adolf Hitler came to power, he demanded that he and the Nazi government of the Third Reich should have authority over the church and its preaching. The German church polarised into two factions: the 'German Christians', who believed the church should respond positively to National Socialism, and the 'Confessing Church' – including such writers as Karl Barth and Dietrich Bonhoeffer – who believed that the church was answerable to Jesus Christ, and him alone. Representatives of this 'Confessing Church' met at Barmen in 1934, where they issued the famous 'Barmen Declaration', perhaps one of the finest statements of the Lordship of Jesus Christ over his church and its implications:

'I am the way, and the truth and the life. No-one comes to the Father except through me.' (John 14:6). 'I tell you the truth, the man who does not enter the sheep pen by the gate, but climbs in by some other way, is a thief and a robber . . . I am the gate; whoever enters through me will be saved' (John 10:1, 9).

Jesus Christ, as he is attested for us in Holy Scripture, is the one Word of God which we have to hear and which we have to trust and obey in life and in death. We reject the false doctrine, that the church could and would have to acknowledge as a source of its proclamation, apart from and besides this one Word of God, still other events and powers, figures and truths, as God's revelation.

In other words, the church cannot and must not substitute anything (for example, the state government or German culture) or anyone (such as Adolf Hitler) for Jesus Christ. If the church ever loses her faithful obedience to her Lord, she has lost her life and her soul.

Doctrine thus defines who we are to obey. It draws a firm line of demarcation between a false church, which answers to the pressures of the age, and a true church, which is obedient and responsible to God, as he has revealed himself in Jesus Christ. 'True knowledge of God is born out of obedience' (John Calvin). Inattention to doctrine robs a church of her reason for existence, and opens the way to enslavement and oppression by the world. The German Christians, through well-intentioned but muddled attitudes towards the world, allowed that world to conquer them. A church which takes doctrine seriously is a church which is obedient to and responsible for what God has entrusted to it. Doctrine gives substance and weight to what the Christian church has to offer to the world. A church which despises or neglects doctrine comes perilously close to losing its reason for existence, and may simply lapse into a comfortable conformity with the world – or whatever part of the world it happens to feel most at home with. Its agenda is set by the world; its presuppositions are influenced by the world; its outlook mirrors that of the world. There are few more pathetic sights than a church wandering aimlessly from one 'meaningful' issue to another in a desperate search for relevance in the eyes of the world.

To speak of obedience may seem to represent some sort of lapse into mindless authoritarianism, or degeneration into blind servility. Obedience may take the form of such slavishness; it need not, and should not. To be a slave to the truth is to maintain intellectual rigour and integrity; to take liberties with the truth is to prefer an imagined and invented state of affairs to reality. If I were to insist that the American Declaration of Independence took place in 1789, despite all the evidence which unequivocally points to the year 1776, I could expect no commendations for maintaining my intellectual freedom or personal integrity. I would simply be obstinately and stubbornly *wrong*, incapable of responding to evidence which demanded a truthful decision.

An obedient response to truth is a mark of intellectual integrity. It marks a willingness to hear what purports to be the truth, to judge it, and, if it is found to be true, to accept it willingly. Truth demands to be accepted, because it inherently deserves to be accepted – and acted upon. Christianity recognises a close link between faith and obedience – witness Paul's profound phrase, 'the obedience of faith' (Rom. 1:5; see pp. 77–8) – making it imperative that the ideas which underlie and give rise to attitudes and actions should be judged, and found to be right.

Beliefs are important because they claim to describe the way things are. They assert that they declare the truth about reality. But beliefs are not just ideas absorbed by our minds, which have no further effect upon us. They affect what we do and what we feel. They influence our hopes and fears. They determine the way we behave. A Japanese fighter pilot of

the Second World War might believe that destroying the
enemies of his emperor ensured his immediate entry into
paradise – and, as many US Navy personnel discovered
to their cost, this belief expressed itself in quite definite
actions. Such pilots had no hesitation in launching suicide
attacks on American warships. Doctrines are ideas – but
they are more than mere ideas. They are the foundation
of our understanding of the world and our place within it.

Doctrine is not, however, something which we have
invented. It is our response to the action of God. Doctrine
is a human mental reaction to the historical action of God.
It is not some sort of speculative guesswork about God or
Christ. Rather, it is rational reflection upon the death and
resurrection of Jesus Christ, in the full awareness of the
newness and mystery of this event. To use a marvellous
turn of phrase from St Paul, it is our 'reasonable service
(*logike latreia*)' to God (Rom. 12:1; note that translations
of the Greek vary). It is responsible, in the sense that it
answers and is answerable to someone. It *answers* to God,
in that it arises in the aftermath of our awareness of being
called, being summoned, by God, through Jesus Christ. We
need to be told what God is like; left to our own devices – as
history makes abundantly clear – a myriad of contradictory
and inconsistent ideas of God would arise, all the products
of human imagination and guesswork. It is *answerable* to
God, in that it purports to speak of him, to describe him,
and to lead to him. For a human to dare to speak about
God in this way is potentially presumptuous, even fatuous
– unless we have reason to believe that we are *authorised*
to speak in this way by God himself.

The notion of 'authority' evokes negative reactions from
many people. It is frequently confused with 'authoritarianism'. In 1950, a work was published entitled *The Authoritarian Personality*, arguing that authoritarianism was the
hallmark of a basically weak and dependent individual,
lacking any personal strengths of character, who compensates for his or her near-total inadequacy by imposing a

mindless authority. 'Authority' is thus often understood as a demand for blind obedience, characteristic of the weak. But authority is not the opposite of freedom. Indeed, rightly understood, authority can actually establish freedom. The real contradiction of authority is *an absence of any account-ability for our actions*. Authority is about being called to answer for one's freedom. Authority is about *accountability*, about being *answerable* to others outside our situation for whatever course of action we freely choose. To speak of the 'authority of God' in this doctrinal context is to stress that we are accountable for the manner in which we respond to him and represent him. We are free to speak about God in whatever way we choose – but *responsible* talk about God is grounded in an awareness of our need to answer to God for what we speak about him.

In part, Christian doctrine seeks to tell the truth about God by exposing false ways of thinking and speaking about God. It shows up much human thinking of God as intellectual Towers of Babel – things which humans have created, in defiance of God. It condemns as false and untrue our sentimental views of Jesus, our cosy ideas about human nature, and slick and too-easy concepts of God. These are exposed as our own creations; we are asked instead to consider God as he has made himself known, however disturbing and disruptive this may prove to be. If doctrine is not grounded in the truth of God, it is to be ridiculed and rejected. Yet the obstinate fact remains, that doctrine claims to be grounded in God's revelation of himself, in the scripturally-mediated account of the coming of Jesus Christ. It declares that it is not a human invention, but a response to the revelation of God. God, it affirms, has permitted – has *authorised* – us to speak about him in this way.

To speak about Jesus Christ is to speak about newness. Far from providing some useful comments on the way things are, Jesus Christ opens up a new way of being. It is this new wine, this new creation, which demands a new way of speaking about God, and what he has done for us. The life, death and resurrection of Jesus Christ bring us a new *knowledge* of God and of ourselves, set firmly in the context of a new *relationship* to God, made possible through faith in Christ. As Christians seek to share with the world their experience of the redeeming and liberating love of God, they are forced to give an account of this experience. How did it happen? What effects did it have? And what are its consequences?

Doctrine thus arises from the passionate commitment of the Christian church to tell the truth about God, and show up the weakness and poverty of non-Christian understandings of who God is and what he is like on the one hand, and who human beings are on the other. Doctrine confronts the world in judgement, and provides a basis for resistance to its oppression. Its starting point was not a smoke-saturated committee room, filled with academics arguing endlessly and pointlessly over their ideas about God. Rather, it begins from a realisation of what God has done for us in Jesus Christ. It begins from an awareness that Christ confronts us, as he confronted his contemporaries, with divine judgement and, in its wake, the possibility of divine renewal. Jesus Christ brings judgement and conversion; in short, he is the Saviour.

And this must have puzzled the first Christians. Indeed, there is every reason for thinking that they were overawed, astonished, and perplexed (as well as overjoyed) at what God had done in and through Jesus Christ. They were acutely aware that there was only one God, and that he jealously reserved use of the word 'saviour' for himself (see, for example, Isa. 45:21–2). Only God can save. The New Testament, however, proclaimed Jesus Christ as Saviour. New Testament texts making this suggestion include Matthew 1:21 (which speaks of Jesus saving his people from their sins), Luke 2:11 (the famous Christmas message of the angels: 'Today in the town of David a Saviour has been born to you'), Acts 4:12 (which affirms that salvation comes through Jesus), Hebrews 2:10 (which calls Jesus the 'author of salvation'). Titus 1:3–4 speaks of 'God our Saviour' at one point, and 'Christ Jesus our Saviour' at another. A contradiction seemed to have developed.

Nevertheless, the first Christians obviously felt that it was vitally important to remain faithful to their experience of salvation through Jesus Christ. Instead of shrugging their shoulders and avoiding facing the issues raised, they asked a crucial question. 'What must be true of Jesus Christ if this is possible?' If Christ is our Saviour, yet salvation is something which God, and God alone can do, it is clear that a very important insight into the identity of Jesus Christ lies to hand. They were determined to tell the truth about Jesus Christ; part of that truth involved wrestling with the implications of what God was acknowledged to have done through him. The doctrine of the incarnation – the declaration that Jesus Christ is both God and man – may be regarded as the climax of the Christian attempt to tell the whole truth about Christ. And this doctrine undergirds the basic Christian conviction that to tell the truth about Jesus Christ is to tell the truth about God – and about ourselves.

This might seem to raise an alarming possibility. Is this emphasis upon Jesus Christ justified? Surely God may be known in other ways? Can God not be seen in a beautiful sunset? Can he not be known through our being deeply impressed by the star-spangled heavens? Can we not sense his presence in the glory of great music, or discern him through a great work of art? But this emphasis upon Jesus Christ is not intended to imply that God cannot be seen anywhere else. It is to declare that God is to be known definitively, most reliably, and most fully through Jesus Christ. The doctrine of the incarnation lends weight to this central Christian insight: that God has chosen to reveal himself supremely and definitively – to the point of becoming incarnate – in Jesus Christ.

To put this another way: Jesus Christ is the authoritative self-revelation of God. The word 'authoritative' is helpful here. Sometimes people speak of a particular performance of a drama (shall we say, Shakespeare's *Macbeth*) or a musical composition (perhaps a Beethoven symphony) as *authoritative*. What is meant by this? The basic idea is that, in some way, this performance conveys what the writer or composer intended far more accurately than its rivals. It is more authentic than the alternatives. It is more reliable. This is not to say that all other performances fail totally to convey anything of what Shakespeare or Beethoven intended – it is to suggest that they fail to convey it in its fullness. They are overshadowed by the authoritative version. They are judged in relation to it. Where they are seen to echo and fulfil his intentions, they are to be praised; where they fail to do justice to them, they are found wanting. By defining one version as authoritative, a benchmark or standard is being established by which all others are to be evaluated.

In the same way, Jesus Christ is an authoritative revelation of God himself. God may indeed be discerned elsewhere – in the wonders of his creation, or in the heights of human artistic creativity. But these are subordinate to the supreme focus of God's self-revelation in Christ. Every now and then, someone suggests that a piece of sixteenth-century verse, or a hitherto obscure drama of the period, was written by none other than Shakespeare himself. And such claims have to be put to the test. How is this done? By examining works which were unquestionably written by Shakespeare, in order that points of similarity may be identified. The works which are known to be authentic are the standard by which others are evaluated. In the same way, Jesus Christ is the authentic revelation of God, by which other alleged revelations can be judged.

Doctrine makes truth-claims. To speak of doctrine as 'truth' is rightly to draw attention to the fundamental Christian conviction that doctrine claims to make significant and justifiable statements about the order of things, about the way things are. Nevertheless, it is also concerned with maintaining the possibility of *encountering* the truth, which the Christian tradition firmly locates in Jesus Christ as the source of her identity. At the outbreak of the Second World War,

William Temple – then Archbishop of York – identified the tension between these concepts of truth in his remark, 'our task with this world is not to explain it, but to convert it.' Although Temple's phrase is clearly derivative (borrowing from Karl Marx), the point he scores is important. Doctrine does not merely describe the way things are – it opens up the possibility of changing them. It is not a static representation, but an invitation to the dynamic transformation, of the human situation. Doctrine is able to effect what it signifies.

Doctrine describes what Christians believe to be true; it also invites those outside the Christian church to believe in this truth. In his *Unscientific Postscript*, the nineteenth-century Danish philosopher Søren Kierkegaard stressed that 'the possibility of knowing what Christianity is without being a Christian must be affirmed.' In other words, it is possible to *know about* Christianity without being a Christian. For Kierkegaard, doctrine is not just a description of what Christianity is. It is also a challenge to *become* a Christian.

Doctrine arises within the community of faith, as it seeks to make sense and give order and structure to its experience of and encounter with God through the risen Christ. Doctrine is thus an 'insider' phenomenon, reflecting the faith of Christian believers in Jesus Christ. Outside this context, doctrine may seem barren and lifeless, in that its vital links with the death and resurrection of Jesus Christ are not fully understood. To those outside the community of faith, what requires explanation and elaboration is not actually specific *doctrines*, but what doctrine attempts and purports to represent – the Christian experience of the risen Christ as Lord. Before doctrine can become meaningful to those outside the Christian church, they must share the Christian experience of the risen Christ. It is difficult to explain the doctrine of the incarnation (to take a particularly important example) to those who are not Christians, because they find it difficult to understand *why* anyone should want to speak of Jesus as both God and man in the first place. The pressures which lead to the doctrine are not fully grasped. Doctrine must therefore be and become a stimulus to evangelism – that is, an attempt to enable those outside the Christian faith to share in its experience and knowledge of God in Jesus Christ.

The foundation of Christian doctrine is thus – and always has been – Jesus Christ. He *is* the truth which sets us free (John 14:6; 8:32). But how do we know about him? How do we have access to this foundational resource of Christian belief? To ask such questions is to move on to deal with the relation of doctrine to Scripture.

3   RESPONDING TO GOD: DOCTRINE AND REVELATION

Christian faith and Christian doctrine are both a response to God. They are a reaction to the action of God. For Christian theology and spirituality, that action of God culminates in the coming of Jesus Christ. One of the most cherished insights of Christian theology is that Jesus Christ represents God addressing us as human persons in and through a human person. Faith is a response to the call of God – an awareness of being called, and a willingness to respond to that call.

'Scripture is the manger in which Christ is laid' (Martin Luther). With these words, Luther points to the centrality of Scripture: there is no other witness to the call of God through the life, death and resurrection of Jesus Christ than this. If Christian doctrine is the response of the Christian church to Jesus Christ, the centrality of Scripture to Christian faith and doctrine will be evident. There is no other way of gaining access to the history of Jesus Christ. The authority of Scripture thus rests partly in its witness to Jesus Christ. But Scripture contains more than an account of the history of Jesus Christ. It tells us how the first Christians understood him – who they thought he was, and what effect they believed this must have on their lives.

The coming of Jesus Christ did not take place in a vacuum. It was not some kind of bolt from the blue, a totally unexpected event. The Old Testament provides us with vital clues about the sort of expectations the people of God had concerning their future Messiah. It allows us to get a feeling of the sense of anticipation felt by the Jewish people as they awaited the coming of their deliverer. The Old Testament writers speak powerfully and movingly of a God who created the world, who called the people of Israel into existence to be his witness to the Gentiles, and who would come again to visit and redeem his people. It is a moving testimony to the active presence of God in the life of a people, and to their conviction that this presence would assume new and more powerful forms in the future. The Old Testament thus matters profoundly to Christians, partly because it sets the coming of Jesus Christ in its proper context. It sets the scene for understanding what the titles applied by the New Testament to Jesus, such as 'Saviour' and 'Messiah', actually mean. To stress that doctrine is a response to the coming of Jesus Christ is thus in no way to set aside the Old Testament. To understand Jesus Christ is to view him against the pattern of divine activity and fidelity established by the Old Testament.

Scripture witnesses to the revelation of God. As such, it is the central resource of Christian faith and doctrine. This stress upon the doctrinal authority and importance of Scripture is the common heritage of all Christians, not merely those who approve of the sixteenth-century Reformation. The Second Vatican Council's dogmatic constitution on divine revelation may be regarded as summarising a consensus amongst responsible Christian theologians concerning the importance and authority of Scripture:

> Since everything asserted by the inspired authors or sacred writers must be held to be asserted by the Holy Spirit, it follows that the books of Scripture must be acknowledged as teaching firmly, faithfully and without error that truth which God wanted put into the sacred writings for the sake of our salvation.

But what, it may reasonably be asked, of other resources for Christian doctrine? What about tradition? Isn't it somehow very *Protestant* to place such emphasis upon the importance of Scripture? These questions demand to be considered before we go any further.

DOCTRINE, TRADITION AND SCRIPTURE

Tradition, rightly understood, is not a source of revelation in addition to Scripture, but a particular way of understanding Scripture which the Christian church has recognised as responsible and reliable. For Irenaeus, a second-century writer especially concerned with the threat posed by Gnosticism, the idea that God could reveal himself authoritatively apart from Scripture was irresponsible. If this was the case, anyone (especially Gnostics!) could claim that they had access to special insights, directly given to them by God. For Irenaeus, God had revealed himself perfectly well in Scripture, and no additional resources were necessary.

But then there was the question of how Scripture was to be interpreted. The Gnostics had a habit of interpreting certain biblical passages in a thoroughly unchristian manner. To combat this, Irenaeus laid down a basic principle. The Christian church interpreted these disputed passages in certain specific ways, which were 'traditional'. In other words, there was a traditional way of reading and interpreting Scripture, reflected in the creeds. To be a Christian was to accept the authority of Scripture in the first place, and in the second to accept that it had to be read in certain ways. Scripture and tradition are thus not two alternative sources of revelation, as suggested in some quarters; rather they are (to use a word favoured by scholars) *coinherent*. Scripture cannot be read as if it had never been read before. There are certain ways of reading Scripture which are more authentically Christian than others.

Tradition is thus rightly understood (as it was understood by both the Reformers and the Second Vatican Council) as a history of interpreting and wrestling with Scripture.

(Reacting against the growing influence of Protestantism in the sixteenth century, some Roman Catholic theologians at this time developed the idea that there were two sources of revelation – Scripture, and unwritten traditions, possessed only by the true church. This has not, however, found sympathy with many twentieth-century Catholic writers.) Tradition is a willingness to read Scripture, taking into account the ways in which it has been read in the past. It is an awareness of the communal dimension of Christian faith, which calls shallow individualism into question. There is more to the interpretation of Scripture than any one individual can discern. It is a willingness to give full weight to the views of those who have gone before us in the faith.

It may be objected at this point, that this seems to contradict the Reformation Scripture principle – that it is Scripture alone which is authoritative. But this principle was never intended by writers such as Luther or Calvin to mean that Scripture is read individualistically. It was in no way intended to elevate the private judgement of an individual above the communal judgement of the church (although it was interpreted in this way by certain radical reformers, outside the mainstream of the Reformation). Rather, the Scripture principle affirms that traditional ways of reading Scripture must, in principle, be open to being checked concerning their reliability. It is possible that the church may occasionally get Scripture wrong (as the Reformers believed that it had been misunderstood at a series of points) – and at these points, it is essential that Scripture be examined in depth to ascertain its true meaning. But that is a matter for the community of faith, not some private individual acting on his or her own behalf.

Tradition, then, is the corporate historical reflection upon Scripture, not a source of revelation in addition to Scripture. It is a process of responsible and obedient reflection upon the meaning of Scripture for the community of faith, in whatever situations it may find itself. It is one of the major achievements of both theological scholarship and the ecumenical movement to demonstrate that this emphasis upon the priority of Scripture is not a Protestant obsession, but is rather a common feature of responsible Christian thought.

DOCTRINE AND THE INTERPRETATION OF SCRIPTURE

Scripture is thus the primary source for doctrinal reflection within the Christian church. There is no other access to the self-revelation of God in Jesus Christ. Many eighteenth-century writers believed that reason was a sort of omnipotent and objective human ability to discover God, and lay down what he is like, and what he can and cannot do. Revelation, it was argued, was thus quite irrelevant and unnecessary: human reason could find out all it needed to know about God without such external aids. That view is now seriously discredited, with the real limitations placed upon human reason being better understood. There are certain things that human reason is very good at – the field of mathematics, for example. Equally, there are certain things it is not so good at. Unaided reason is no longer regarded as having anything especially helpful to say about who God is and what he is like – although it is invaluable in making sense of God's revelation of himself.

Doctrine interprets Scripture. There is, however, a real danger that biblical interpretation and doctrine will become detached from one another, with doctrine being seen as having an independent existence. This is a seriously deficient understanding of the nature of doctrine. Doctrine claims to interpret Scripture, and is to be judged in that light. It is a framework for the interpretation of Scripture which claims to be based upon Scripture itself. If doctrine is understood as a way of interpreting Scripture on the basis of Scripture, the great Reformation principle, *scriptura est suipsius interpres* ('Scripture is its own interpreter'), is upheld. The sixteenth-century Reformation is a classic case of doctrine being subjected to radical examination, to see whether it was, in fact, firmly based in Scripture. Reformers such as Martin Luther and John Calvin were, in principle, prepared to abandon doctrines which could not be shown to be securely grounded in Scripture.

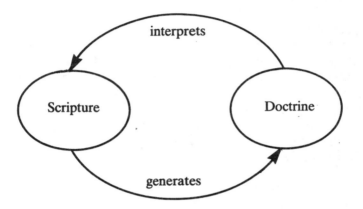

FIGURE 1 The Interaction of Scripture and Doctrine

Perhaps the best way of summarising the relationship between doctrine and scriptural interpretation is shown in Figure 1. The starting point for doctrinal reflection is an attempt to make sense of the scriptural witness to God's saving action towards us, culminating in the coming of Jesus Christ. The resulting doctrines are not an end in themselves; rather, they are themselves a framework for the interpretation of Scripture. There is a process of feedback between doctrine and Scripture, as they mutually comple-ment one another. The primary purpose of doctrine is to allow a more reliable interpretation and application of Scrip-ture. This basic approach can be found in John Calvin's famous *Institutes of the Christian Religion* (1559), in which the distinguished reformer sets out to provide his readers with a volume of Christian doctrine which will aid them as they read Scripture.

> Although the Holy Scriptures contain a perfect doctrine, to which nothing can be added (our Lord having been pleased to unfold the infinite treasures of his wisdom therein), every person who is not intimately acquainted with them needs some sort of guidance and direction, as to what he or she ought to look for in them . . . Hence it is the duty of those who have received from God more light than others to assist the simple in this manner and, as it were, give them a helping hand to guide and assist them to find everything that God has been pleased to teach us in his word. Now, the best way of doing this is to deal systematically with all the main themes of Christian philosophy.

In other words, a systematic presentation of the main themes of Christian doctrine is an excellent guide to Scripture. It provides a sort of route map by which the various scriptural landmarks may be located and identified, and related to each other. Doctrine, to use a phrase due to Calvin, is like a pair of spectacles through which Scripture may be properly read. It stresses the unity of Scripture, which might otherwise seem like a series of unconnected stories and sayings.

A helpful way of thinking of the relation of doctrine to Scripture, probably suggested by a growing Victorian public interest in botanical gardens, was put forward by the nineteenth-century Scottish writer Thomas Guthrie. Guthrie argued that Scripture is like nature, in which flowers and plants grow freely in their natural habitat, unordered by human hands. The human desire for orderliness leads to these same plants being collected and arranged in botanical gardens according to their species, in order that they can be individually studied in more detail. The same plants are found in different contexts – one of which is natural, the other of which is the result of human ordering. Doctrine represents the human attempt to order the ideas of Scripture, arranging them in a logical manner in order that their mutual relation can be better understood.

Doctrine integrates scriptural statements. It brings together the kaleidoscope of scriptural affirmations about God, Jesus Christ and human nature. It discerns common patterns underlying the wealth of scriptural statements and illustrations. It distills the essence of these statements into as compact a form as possible. Doctrine is thus a summary of Scripture. Suppose you were asked to explain what Christians believed about Jesus Christ. You might well find that this might take you some time. You would probably want to talk about the main New Testament titles used to refer to Jesus – such as 'Son of God', 'Son of Man', 'Saviour' and 'Lord'. You would find yourself trying to explain what each of them meant, and what it told us about Jesus. You might want to take a series of key scriptural verses, each making an important affirmation about the importance of Jesus – such as Romans 1:3–4, with its succinct explanation of what the resurrection tells us about his identity. Yet you could not summarise the entire biblical witness to Jesus Christ in a single proof text.

After a while, you might find yourself wondering if there was an easier way of doing this. Is there any way in which the rich (and very extensive) scriptural witness to the identity and importance of Jesus Christ could be summarised in a sentence or two? The doctrinal statement 'Jesus is God and man' aims to do this. It provides a neat outline of the key features of the Christian understanding of the identity and significance of Jesus Christ. It is a summary of the scriptural teaching, and not a substitute for it.

As an example, let us consider the doctrine of the incarnation – the idea that God became man in Jesus Christ. What scriptural elements does it integrate? Even the briefest of lists of such scriptural elements would include:

- the belief that God has acted decisively for human salvation through Jesus Christ.
- the belief that God has revealed himself definitively in the person of Jesus Christ.
- the practice of the worship of Jesus, already found within the New Testament, and a key feature of Christian devotion thereafter.

The doctrine of the incarnation distills the common features of each of these elements. It asks the question: What must be true about Jesus Christ if these beliefs and practices are justified?

A second example might be the doctrine of the Trinity, which attempts to bring together into a single formula the richness of the Christian understanding of God. For example, it holds together the following central elements of the biblical witness to the nature and purposes of God:

- God created the world.
- God redeemed us through Jesus Christ.
- God is present in his church through the Spirit.

The doctrine of the Trinity affirms that these all relate to the same God. It is not as if one god created the world, while another redeemed it, and a third is present thereafter. Rather, the same God is present and active throughout the history of redemption. The doctrine integrates these three elements into a greater whole. Each is declared to be an essential aspect of the Christian understanding of God. It is not meant to explain how God can be like this; it simply affirms that, according to the biblical witness, he *is* like this. It insists that the biblical statements about God be seen as an integrated whole, rather than a series of loosely collected items.

Seen in this way, doctrine is not – and was never meant to be – a substitute for Scripture. Rather, it is a learning aid for reading Scripture. (A learning aid, it may be added, that can be corrected in the light of Scripture, if it can be shown to be out of line with it.) Like a pair of spectacles, it brings the text of Scripture into focus, allowing us to notice things which might otherwise be missed. Doctrine is always under Scripture, its servant rather than its master. Doctrine stands or falls with the Word of God, revealed in Scripture, in that this Word of God precedes, creates and criticises all doctrinal statements.

DOCTRINE AND THE NARRATIVE OF SCRIPTURE

Recent discussion on the relation between doctrine and Scripture has highlighted a problem which, despite its difficulty and technicality, demands to be considered in the present chapter. The following quotation from *Believing in the Church*, published in 1981 by the Doctrine Commission of the Church of England, identifies this problem:

> The form of Scripture is not such that we can easily deduce from it general statements of what it is that we believe. Its most characteristic mode of writing is that of narrative . . . it contains relatively little of the kind of doctrinal statement from which a reasoned presentation of the Christian faith could be logically deduced . . . The characteristic mode in which Scripture conveys to us the things concerning God, Jesus and man is not (in this sense) 'doctrinal' at all. It is mainly (though not exclusively) *narrative*.

In other words, Scripture is primarily concerned to tell us the story of God's redeeming engagement with the world, culminating in the life, death and resurrection of Jesus Christ. It relates a history.

So how do we make the transition from history to doctrine? How do we convert a story into a belief? Two questions are of central importance. First, how can a story, a narrative, be *authoritative*? And second, how can a narrative or story be converted into doctrine? We begin with the first of these two questions.

To see how a story can be authoritative, let us turn to the late Renaissance, and the city of Florence. Florence went through a series of political and social difficulties in the late Renaissance, with a resulting loss of morale. It found itself plagued by internal factionalisation and external threat. How could it make sense of what was happening to it?

The answer lay in noticing parallels between the history of Florence and that of ancient Rome. The Florentines noticed that Rome seemed to suffer from much the same difficulties as they did. The story of Rome seemed to tie in with the story of Florence. It cast light on what was happening. Gradually, the story of Rome began to be recognised as being authoritative for Florence. The story of ancient Rome was seen as the best way of making sense of what was happening in modern Florence. In trying to understand their present problems, the pattern of the past was seen to be helpful.

In a similar way, the story of Jesus Christ is held to be authoritative for Christians. It is this story, and no other, which helps to make sense of the riddles of human faith and experience. And whereas Florence had to invent its links with ancient Rome, the Christian church stands in an unbroken line with the story of Jesus – a story which is recalled regularly in the eucharistic celebration. The character of the Christian community arises from the fact that it came into being as a response to Jesus Christ. The narrative of Jesus is recognised as authoritative by the Christian church. Its attitudes to power, to pride, to loss, to death, to grief, to despair – all are governed by the narrative of Jesus Christ. It evokes a deep sense of 'happening', the memory of a foundational narrative and its present significance for the community whose identity is tightly bound up with it. It provides a focus of identity for the community. The New Testament affirmation of the conformity of the believer to

Christ – that, through faith, those who believe in Christ are somehow caught up in him, so that *his* history becomes *their* history – provides a significant theological foundation for this correlation of narratives. His death is their death, his life is their life – and the narrative of Jesus gives some specification to Christian existence by aligning that existence with a lived life, with a specific historical person.

The story of Jesus Christ controls the Christian self-understanding. Especially in the Pauline writings, participation in Christ points to a conformity of the believer's existence to his. Through faith, the believer is caught up in a new outlook on life, a new structure of existence, embodied in Jesus Christ. Through faith, we come to share in Christ. His story becomes our story. The believer is one who is 'in Christ'. For Paul, the believer repeats the story of Jesus Christ in his or her own life, sharing in that story: we share in his sufferings, in order that we may share in glory (Rom. 8:17). The story of Jesus Christ gives some shape, specification and substance to what human outlooks on life, what forms of action, what moral motivations, are appropriate expressions of our own sharing in the life of Christ.

In this way, the history of Jesus Christ is authoritative within the Christian church. It is this story, and no other, which controls our understanding of God, Jesus Christ, and ourselves. It is the story of Jesus, for example, which governs Christian ethics: in the life of Jesus, we see a pattern of faithful and obedient response to God which is the goal of all believers.

This line of argument helps us see how a story can be authoritative. We must now turn to the second problem. How can a story give rise to doctrines? To deal with this question, let us go back to Ancient Greece. Early Greek thinkers tended to use stories as a way of making sense of the world, and discovering more about it. The Greek myths are basically stories or narratives (whose truth content, it may be added, was virtually non-existent; the gospel story, on the other hand, is thoroughly grounded in history). To explain things, you told a story. A decisive shift appears to have taken place shortly before the time of Plato. A conceptual way of thinking now gained the upper hand. Ideas took the place of stories. In the modern period, conceptual ways of thinking tend to dominate western culture, while narrative ways of thinking are dominant in native African cultures.

These ways of thinking are not inconsistent. The gospel is capable of being stated in both forms – the story of Jesus Christ, and the interpretation of this story in terms of doctrines. The story of Jesus takes priority, however. Doctrine provides the framework by which the scriptural narrative is interpreted. It is not an arbitrary framework, however, but one which is suggested by that narrative, and intimated by Scripture itself. It is to be discerned within, rather than imposed upon, that narrative. The narrative is primary, and the interpretative framework secondary. The New Testament includes both the narrative of Jesus of Nazareth and interpretation of the relevance of that narrative for the existence of the first Christian communities. Doctrine represents the extension of the doctrinal hints, markers and signposts to be found within the New Testament, especially in the Pauline writings.

Narratives need interpretation. The scriptural narrative is no exception. The Old Testament could be read as a story of the quest for identity among a nomadic people of the Ancient Near East. The Gospels could be read as the story of a misguided Galilean revolutionary or a radical Jewish rabbi. But these would not be especially reliable ways of reading the scriptural story. Doctrine lays down the right way of reading this story. It affirms the particular interpretation, or range of interpretations, of the scriptural narrative appropriate for the Christian community. Thus the assertion 'Jesus is the Christ' is a doctrinal statement which allows the story of Jesus to be read and understood in a particular way – the *right* way, according to Christianity. Other ways certainly exist (for example, reading the story of Jesus as the story of a purely human political figure) – doctrine declares that these are at best inadequate, and at worst wrong.

As we noted earlier, Calvin suggested that doctrine was like a pair of spectacles for reading Scripture. Doctrine, like spectacles, brings things into focus and allows a clearer vision of things than the unaided eye. Doctrine is thus a way of reading Scripture, suggested by Scripture itself, which brings the text into focus, and allows us to read it with greater clarity. For example, Romans 1:3–4 justifies Paul's claim that Jesus is the Son of God by appealing to the story of Jesus. Two crucial elements of that story – his descent from David, and his resurrection – are seen as establishing that Jesus is the Son of God. Once this doctrinal insight has been reached, the scriptural story can be read again *in the light of that insight*. This pattern is repeated throughout Paul's writings. The story of Jesus allows insights into the nature of God, Jesus and humanity, which can then be used to make further sense of the scriptural narrative. The crucial point is this: the doctrines which interpret the story of Jesus are themselves based upon that story. They are not plucked out of thin air.

An example may make this point clearer. The doctrine of the incarnation affirms two vital insights: 'Jesus is God' and 'Jesus is man'. Whatever else these insights may mean, they mean that, within the scriptural story of Jesus Christ, Jesus may be seen playing two quite different roles – the human and the divine. Two roles which had hitherto been regarded as mutually exclusive, demanding different actors, are held by the narrative to be intimately related and focused on the single person of Jesus. Within the context of the narrative, Jesus acts as God (for example, by forgiving sin: Mark 2:5–7), as well as man (for example, by weeping or by becoming tired). The doctrine of the two natures provides a means of interpreting the scriptural narrative, and ensuring its internal consistency. There is thus a dynamic relationship between doctrine and the scriptural narrative. There is a process of interaction, of *feedback*, between doctrine and

Scripture, between the interpretative framework and the narrative itself.

The only major difficulty which could result from going over from a narrative to a conceptual framework of thinking would arise if the original narrative were lost. Suppose that the story of Jesus Christ, having being allowed to generate a doctrinal specific framework, were forgotten. The doctrines remained, but the narrative was forgotten. Had this occurred, serious anxiety would necessarily have resulted concerning the reliability of this framework. It would have been left suspended without visible support. There would be no way of checking whether the doctrines were reliable interpretations of the story of Jesus Christ. However, the foundational narrative of Jesus has been preserved by the community of faith, and accorded primary status in doctrinal reflection (particularly within the churches of the Reformation). The Scripture principle is basically an assertion of the primacy of the scriptural narrative of Jesus over any doctrines which it may generate. The scriptural narrative remains, and we thus continue to have access to a means of testing the reliability of doctrines. Doctrine does not have an existence which is independent of Scripture; rather, doctrine is always under Scripture. In principle, doctrines will always continue to be judged on the basis of whether they reliably interpret the biblical witness to Jesus Christ.

Earlier, we noted a misgiving many people have about doctrine. Doctrines may at times seem abstract, and not firmly located in the reality of everyday life. Yet the realisation that doctrine is basically the interpretation of a story – the history of Jesus Christ – brings home the fact that doctrine is firmly grounded in the realities of life. Doctrine is a bridge, which seeks to link our lives with the life of Jesus Christ. It aims to connect the realities of *our* existence with the realities of *his* existence. It interprets *our* story in the light of *his* story. Doctrine is only to be dismissed as an abstract irrelevance if its purpose and place are seriously misunderstood.

The parables of Jesus also make doctrinal statements in the form of stories. A story is told, and the doctrine is explained. What might be seen as abstract and unreal (the doctrine) is shown to be grounded in the concrete events of human existence. For example, the Pauline doctrine of justification by faith seems to many to be something of an unintelligible abstraction. Yet this doctrine merely states in a conceptual form the same basic point made so memorably and so powerfully in the parable of the Pharisee and the Publican (Luke 18:9–14). The utter paradox of grace is here stated with supreme clarity. It is not the morally upright Pharisee but the repentant sinner who is justified before God. (Note that there is not a hint of hypocrisy here; the Pharisee would have done all that he claimed to have done. To suggest that the Pharisee was a liar is to lose sight of the point of the parable.) The doctrine of justification by faith makes much the same point as the parable. Yet the neatness and conceptual clarity of the doctrine is offset by the vividness of the parable, and its firm location in the world of human life. Perhaps we need to recapture the ability and will to restate doctrines in terms of stories, if their power, relevance and vitality are to be fully appreciated.

This, then, is a very brief sketch of how the story of Jesus Christ can give rise to doctrine. There is no inconsistency or major difficulty involved. Indeed, there is an enormous advantage to this relation of narrative and doctrine: it means that Christianity can make sense to anyone, whether they use narrative (for example, in many modern African cultures) or conceptual ways of thinking (for example, in modern western cultures). The gospel can be stated in ways appropriate for all, whether their worlds are shaped by stories or by ideas.

This chapter may have conveyed the idea that doctrine is primarily about ideas – ideas derived from Scripture, to be sure, but ideas nevertheless. This might create the impression that doctrine is rather stuffy and dull, having no bearing upon human experience. In fact, Christian doctrine is a vital resource in understanding and transforming human experience. We shall explore how in the following chapter.

4 INTELLECT AND FEELINGS: DOCTRINE AND EXPERIENCE

Christianity represents a judicious compromise between two extreme views, one subjective, one objective. On the one hand, there is the extreme represented by a purely emotional faith, which experiences God and trusts implicitly in him – but is unable to express itself coherently. This approach is totally subjective, reducing faith to little more than a muddled bundle of emotions. This view is inadequate, rather than wrong; it needs to be supplemented with a stress on the objective side of faith. We don't just believe in God, we believe certain quite definite things about him. In other words, faith has a content as well as an object. It claims to tell the truth (see chapter 2). It is the task of every generation in the history of the Christian church to develop an articulate and authoritative account of its faith. The believer is also a thinker, and can never permit his faith to remain or become a shallow uninformed emotionalism. Emotion is an important element of the Christian faith, and those who despise it have no right to do so – but on its own, it is inadequate, incapable of doing justice to the essence of Christian faith.

On the other hand, there is the view that Christianity is a list of intellectual propositions to which the believer's assent is demanded. This severely objective approach needs to be corrected by recognising that Christian faith is grounded in experience. Faith does not merely concern beliefs; it concerns life, in every one of its rich aspects. The 'God of the Christians' (to borrow a phrase from the third-century writer Tertullian) is no intellectual abstraction, but a God who is known in and through personal experience. The distinguished theologian Rudolf Bultmann made the point that doctrine without experience is little more than a dead letter:

> If someone says that he cannot find God in the reality of his own existence, and if he tries to make up for this by the thought that God is nevertheless the final cause of everything that exists, then his belief in God is the intellectual speculation of a dogma. No matter how strongly he may hold this belief, it will never be true faith – for faith can only be the recognition of the activity of God in his own life.

Experience of God provides the stimulus to develop doctrines about God. Thus the Christian belief in the divinity of Christ did not arise as an intellectual theory, but through the impact of *experiencing* Jesus Christ as God. The early Christians were thus faced with the intellectual task of thinking through the implications of their experience of Christ as God, and expressing it in as clear and persuasive a manner as possible. The full-blooded nature of Christian faith can never be adequately expressed as propositions.

Although each of these views is correct and important, each is inadequate on its own. It is possible for Christianity to degenerate into little more than an intellectual system, rather than a relationship with a person, who enters into our experience and transforms it. The intellectual side of Christian faith is important – but once more, taken on its own, it is inadequate. A judicious compromise, therefore, is necessary in order to preserve both the subjective and objective aspects of faith – in other words, Christian faith is grounded in experience, but its content may still be summarised in propositions such as 'Jesus is Lord', 'Jesus is the Son of God', or 'Jesus is true God and true man'. There is no inconsistency involved – both the proposition and the experience relate to the same greater reality, which lies behind them both. Faith involves both head and heart. Objective and subjective aspects of faith are like two sides of the same coin – they may be different, but they are both essential aspects of the same thing. They both represent the same thing, viewed from different angles.

There is, however, something of a tension between the objective and subjective aspects of faith. On the one hand, we want to talk about God as the one whom we experience, love and worship in adoration and wonder. On the other, we are only too painfully aware of the simple fact that God is God, and that human language is quite incapable of adequately expressing everything that we want to say about him. The majesty and wonder of God tends to reduce us to silence. Our experience of him is virtually impossible to put into words. But we must speak of God, even though we recognise the inadequacy of our words to do justice either to God himself, or even to our experience of him. How else can we share our experience of him with the world? Words are the only means we have of talking about God.

Suppose that you were to cross the Atlantic Ocean on one of the great liners that still work the transatlantic routes. You would probably find that you were overwhelmed by the immensity of that ocean – by its sheer size, by the sense of being totally insignificant in comparison with its vastness, as you spent day after day without seeing land. Your experience of the ocean would make a very deep impression upon you. Suppose that you subsequently were to pick up a map of the western hemisphere, and find the Atlantic Ocean reduced to nothing more than some printed lines on a piece of paper. You might be fortunate enough to find the ocean coloured blue, and the land masses of America and Europe green – but all that you would have in your hands would be a piece of paper. How would your experience of the Atlantic Ocean relate to this small area of blue colour on that paper?

Two points may be made. First, nobody in their right mind

is going to suggest that the area of blue colour on that map is meant to be an exact representation of the Atlantic Ocean. The map is not *identical* with that vast ocean. Rather, the map is an attempt to indicate how various things are related to one another – for example, where Europe and America are situated in relation to each other, and to the Atlantic Ocean. It is not even an attempt to scale down the ocean so that you can get the same sort of experience you once had, only on a smaller scale – it is meant to convey certain limited (but important!) information, rather than reproduce an authentic experience in all its fullness.

Second, the map is based upon the personal experience of countless others, as they also crossed the Atlantic. Whereas your experience is undoubtedly real and important to you, it represents a single, isolated and very personal impression of a much greater reality. Taken on its own, your experience of the Atlantic Ocean is unreliable, perhaps providing your friends with as much information about you as about the ocean itself.

Furthermore, all of us tend to dismiss the experience of others. We are often unwilling to accept anything on the authority of others. We are very reluctant to allow that others might experience more than we do, or have insights which we overlooked. The noted theologian A. E. Taylor made this point very clearly.

> Authority and experience do not stand over against one another in sharp and irreconcilable opposition. Authority is the self-assertion of the reality of an experience which contains more than any individual has succeeded in analysing and extricating for himself. It is indispensable for us as finite historical beings who need a safeguard against our inveterate tendency to supplement the statement 'this is what I can make of this situation' by the perilous addition, 'and this is all there is to it'.

In other words, one individual's experience is unlikely ever to sound the full depths of reality – but *many* such individuals might, by pooling their experiences, give rise to a much more reliable picture of reality.

The function of the map of the Atlantic Ocean is to combine as many impressions of that ocean as possible, in order that a more reliable picture may be built up. The experiences of others, upon which the map is based, are just as vivid and real as yours – but the map eliminates the personal element of experience of the Atlantic Ocean, in order to provide a more generally reliable guide to the same reality. The parallels between doctrines and maps will be obvious. Doctrines are essentially the distillation of the Christian experience of God, in which countless personal experiences are compared and reduced to their common features. Thus the formula 'true God and true man' is at the very least an attempt to express the conviction that we only know both God and man through Jesus.

Christian doctrine cannot be – and anyway was never meant to be – a substitute for experience of the living God. It is an attempt to relate Jesus Christ to God and to us, as a map relates the Atlantic Ocean to Europe and America. It aims to put Jesus on the map between God and ourselves, in order to allow us to experience God through Jesus. Thus the formula of the creed, which speaks of Jesus as 'true God and true man', is really placing Jesus on a theological map. Just as the map told the traveller that the Atlantic would lead him from Europe to America, from the Old World to the New, so the doctrine of the 'two natures' of Christ tells us that we encounter God through Jesus Christ.

Refugees fleeing to the United States from persecution or a hopeless economic situation in Europe in the first decades of the twentieth century knew that their hope of a new life lay in crossing the Atlantic Ocean. The deep sense of relief and joy when the New York skyline came into view is well known to us through contemporary films. And so it is with those who are seeking for God, for meaning and hope, in a seemingly dark, meaningless and hopeless world. Through Christ, they encounter the living God, the source of their new life, their hope and their joy. Nobody is for one moment suggesting that this is everything that could be said about Jesus, or that it adequately describes the deep personal significance which he holds for each and every believer – but it does help us to begin to locate that significance, to be more precise about it than would otherwise be possible.

Doctrine thus addresses and interprets experience. It aims to make sense of human feelings, by explaining what they mean and what they point to. One such feeling has been explored with considerable brilliance by the great English literary critic and novelist C. S. Lewis, and deserves special attention. Lewis was aware of certain deep human emotions which pointed to a dimension of our existence beyond time and space. There is, Lewis suggested, a deep and intense feeling of longing within human beings, which no earthly object or experience can satisfy. Lewis terms this sense 'joy', and argues that it points to God as its source and goal (hence the title of his autobiography, *Surprised by Joy*). Doctrine interprets this experience as a longing after God. It gives shape and meaning to what might otherwise seem a meaningless aspect of human existence. Doctrine interprets the sense of longing as a pointer towards its fulfilment in a relationship with God.

To understand Lewis at this point, the idea of 'joy' needs to be explained in a little more detail. From the windows of his family home in Belfast, Northern Ireland, the young Lewis could see the distant Castlereagh Hills. The sight of these distant hills, often wrapped in mist, seemed to him to symbolise something which lay beyond his reach. A sense of intense longing arose as he contemplated them. He could not say exactly *what* it was that he longed for; merely that there was a sense of emptiness within him, which the mysterious hills seemed to heighten, without satisfying. In his novel *The Pilgrim's Regress*, Lewis uses the image of these hills as a symbol of the heart's unknown desire.

Lewis describes this experience (perhaps better known

to students of German Romanticism as *Sehnsucht*) in some detail in his autobiography *Surprised by Joy*. He tells his readers how, as a young child, he was standing by a flowering currant bush, when – for some unexplained reason – a distant and poignant memory was triggered off.

> There suddenly arose in me without warning, as if from a depth not of years but of centuries, the memory of that earlier morning at the Old House when my brother had brought his toy garden into the nursery. It is difficult to find words strong enough for the sensation which came over me; Milton's 'enormous bliss' of Eden . . . comes somewhere near it. It was a sensation, of course, of desire; but desire for what? Not, certainly, for a biscuit-tin filled with moss, nor even (though that came into it) for my own past . . . and before I knew what I desired, the desire itself was gone, the whole glimpse withdrawn, the world turned commonplace again, or only stirred by a longing for the longing that had just ceased. It had only taken a moment of time; and in a certain sense everything else that had ever happened to me was insignificant in comparison.

Lewis here describes a brief moment of insight, a devastating moment of feeling caught up in something which goes far beyond the realms of everyday experience. But what did it mean? What, if anything, did it point to?

Lewis addressed this question in a remarkable sermon entitled 'The Weight of Glory', preached at Oxford University on 8 June 1941. Lewis spoke of 'a desire which no natural happiness will satisfy', 'a desire, still wandering and uncertain of its object and still largely unable to see that object in the direction where it really lies'. There is something self-defeating about human desire, in that what is desired, when achieved, seems to leave the desire unsatisfied. Lewis illustrates this from the age-old quest for beauty.

The books or the music in which we thought the beauty was located will betray us if we trust to them; it was not *in* them, it only came *through* them, and what came through them was longing. These things – the beauty, the memory of our own past – are good images of what we really desire; but if they are mistaken for the thing itself they turn into dumb idols, breaking the hearts of their worshippers. For they are not the thing itself; they are only the scent of a flower we have not found, the echo of a tune we have not heard, news from a country we have not visited.

The paradox of hedonism – the simple, yet stultifying, fact that pleasure cannot satisfy – is another instance of this curious phenomenon. Pleasure, beauty, personal relationships: all seem to promise so much, and yet when we grasp them, we find that what we were seeking was not located in them, but lies beyond them. There is a 'divine dissatisfaction' within human experience, which prompts us to ask whether there is anything which may satisfy the human quest to fulfil the desires of the human heart.

Lewis argues that there is. Hunger, he suggests, is an excellent example of a human sensation of needing something, which corresponds to a real physical need. This need points to the existence of food by which it may be met. Thirst is an example of a human longing pointing to a human need, which in turn points to its fulfilment in drinking. Any human longing, he argues, points to a genuine human need, which in turn points to a real object corresponding to that need. A similar point is made, although a little cryptically, in relation to human sexual desire. And so, Lewis suggests, it is reasonable to suggest that the deep human sense of infinite longing which cannot be satisfied by any physical or finite object or person must point to a real human need which can, in some way, be met. Human desire, the deep and bitter-sweet longing for something that will satisfy us, points beyond finite objects and finite persons (who seem able to fulfil this desire, yet eventually prove incapable of doing so); it points *through* these objects, and persons towards their real goal and fulfilment in God himself.

This point is made clearly in a letter to his brother, dated 31 October 1931.

> The 'idea of God' in *some* minds does contain, not a mere abstract definition, but real imaginative perception of goodness and beauty, beyond their own resources, and this not only in minds which already believe in God. It certainly seems to me that the 'vague something' which has been suggested to one's mind as desirable, all one's life, in experiences of nature and music and poetry, even in such ostensibly irreligious forms as the 'land east of the Sun and west of the Moon' in Morris, and which arouses desires that no finite object even pretends to satisfy, can be argued *not* to be any product of our own imagination.

In other words, the sense of 'desires that no finite object even pretends to satisfy' corresponds to a real human need, and the fulfilment of that need – but how?

Lewis argues that this sense of longing points to its origin and its fulfilment in God himself. In this, he echoes a great theme of traditional Christian thinking about the origin and goal of human nature. 'You have made us for yourself, O Lord, and our hearts are restless until they find their rest in you' (Augustine of Hippo). We are made by God, and we experience a deep sense of longing for him, which only he can satisfy. Although Lewis' reflections on the desire he calls 'joy' reflect his personal experience, it is evident that he (and countless others) consider that this sense of longing is a widespread feature of human nature and experience. An important point of contact for the proclamation of the gospel is thus established.

Lewis' insights also bring new depth to familiar biblical passages concerning human longing for God. 'As the deer pants for streams of water, so my soul pants for you, O God. My soul thirsts for God, the living God' (Ps. 42:1–2).

Note the great sense of *longing* for God expressed in this passage – a sense of longing which assumes added meaning if Lewis' reflections on 'joy' are allowed. Note also the biblical parallel between a sense of need – in this case, animal thirst – and the human need of and desire for God.

Perhaps the finest statement of the theological implications of this deep sense of longing is to be found in *Till We Have Faces*, Lewis' brilliant retelling of the classic Greek love story of Cupid and Psyche. In one passage, Lewis has Psyche tell her sister (who here relates the story) of her longing for something which she senses lies beyond the world as she experiences it.

'I have always – at least, ever since I can remember – had a longing for death.'

'Ah, Psyche,' I said, 'have I made you so little happy as that?'

'No, no, no,' she said. 'You don't understand. Not that kind of longing. It was when I was happiest that I longed most. It was on happy days, when we were up there on the hills, the three of us, with the wind and the sunshine . . . Do you remember? The colour and the smell, and looking across at the Grey Mountain in the distance? And because it was so beautiful, it set me longing, always longing. Somewhere else there must be more of it. Everything seemed to be saying, Psyche come! But I couldn't (not yet) come and I didn't know where I was to come to. It almost hurt me. I felt like a bird in a cage when the other birds of its kind are flying home.'

Psyche's experience of a sense of longing for something indefinable, evoked by the beauty of the world, ends in frustration; nothing in the world can satisfy her longing. It is only by being set free from the limitations of the world itself that Psyche can experience the fulfilment of her sense of longing. And so our hearts are also restless, until they find their rest in the God who created us for fellowship with him.

Doctrine aims to interpret experience, in order to transform it, through an encounter with the risen Christ. It is like a net which we can cast over experience, in order to capture its meaning. It interprets the human sense of 'longing' as 'longing *after God*', and thus opens up the way for this longing to be satisfied, and thus transformed.

Sometimes doctrine interprets experience by declaring that it can be unreliable and misleading. Experience appears to suggest one thing; doctrine interprets it to suggest something rather different. One of the most important writers to deal with this point is the great German reformer, Martin Luther. Luther's characteristic approach to the interpretation of experience is often known as 'the theology of the cross'. He suggests that we attempt to imagine what it was like for the disciples on the first Good Friday. They had given up everything to follow Jesus. Their whole reason for living centred on him. He seemed to have the answers to all their questions. Then, in front of their eyes, he was taken from them and publicly executed. You can feel an immense sense of despair as you read the Gospel accounts of the death of Jesus. The moment of Jesus' death would probably have been the darkest point in the lives of the disciples. It must have seemed as if their entire world had collapsed, shown up as a fraud and an illusion.

Of course, we know how that story ended. We know how the disciples' sorrow was transformed to joy and wonder, as the news of the resurrection of Jesus became known. But try to imagine yourself standing among the disciples as they watched Jesus suffer and die – *without* knowing that he would be raised again from the dead. Set aside your knowledge of what happens later, and try to imagine what it must have been like to watch Jesus die on the cross. Where was God in all this? Why didn't he intervene? It was all enough to make anyone doubt whether God existed in the first place. It is easy to get a feel for the sense of despair and bewilderment on that sad day. God was experienced as being absent. There was no way in which anyone experienced his presence on that dreadful day. Even Jesus himself seems to have had a momentary sense of the absence of God – 'My God, my God, why have you forsaken me?' (Matt. 27:46).

This way of thinking brings home to us how unreliable experience and feelings can be as guides to the presence of God. Those around the cross did not experience the presence of God – so they concluded that he was absent from the scene. The resurrection overturns that judgement: God was present in a hidden manner, which experience mistook for his absence. Doctrine interprets our feelings, even to the point of contradicting them when they are misleading. It stresses the faithfulness of God to his promises, and the reality of the resurrection hope – even where experience seems to suggest otherwise. Doctrine thus gives us a framework for making sense of the contradictions of experience.

It is to his credit that C. S. Lewis also considered the way in which words can *generate* experience. In *Surprised by Joy*, he comments on the effect of a few lines of poetry upon his imagination. The lines were from Longfellow's *Saga of King Olaf*: 'I heard a voice that cried,/Balder the beautiful/Is dead, is dead.'

These words had a profound impact upon the young Lewis.

> I knew nothing about Balder; but instantly I was uplifted into huge regions of northern sky, I desired with almost sickening intensity something never to be described (except that it is cold, spacious, severe, pale and remote) and then . . . found myself at the very same moment already falling out of that desire and wishing I were back in it.

Words, Lewis discovered, have the ability to evoke an experience we have not yet had, in addition to describing an experience we are familiar with. In his essay *The Language of Religion*, he made this point as follows:

This is the most remarkable of the powers of Poetic language: to convey to us the quality of experiences which we have not had, or perhaps can never have, to use factors within our experience so that they become pointers to something outside our experience – as two or more roads on a map show us where a town that is off the map must lie. Many of us have never had an experience like that which Wordsworth records near the end of *Prelude* XIII; but when he speaks of 'the visionary dreariness', I think we get an inkling of it.

Doctrine shares this characteristic of poetic language, as identified by Lewis – it tries to convey to us the quality of the Christian experience of God. Doctrine is able to offer some pointers for the benefit of those who have yet to discover what it feels like to experience God. It uses a cluster of key words to try to explain what it is like to know God, by analogy with human experience. Let us take forgiveness: if you can imagine what it feels like to be forgiven for a really serious offence, you can begin to understand the Christian experience of forgiveness. Or reconciliation: if you can imagine the joy of being reconciled to someone who matters very much to you, you can get a glimpse of what the Christian experience of coming home to God is like. It is like coming home after being away and alone for a long time. Doctrine uses analogies like these to try to signpost – like roads leading off Lewis' map to an unseen town – the Christian experience of God, for the benefit of those who have yet to have this transforming experience.

Those who have experienced the reality of God in Christ find that they have been called out of the world. It is true that Christians continue to live in the world. The love of God draws us from the world, in order to send us back into it. Christians are called to be *in* the world, but not *of* the world. This brings us to the fourth aspect of Christian doctrine to be considered in this present work: doctrine marks believers off from the world. It gives Christian individuals and communities a sense of identity in the world. We shall explore these themes in the chapter which follows. If the present chapter is concerned with the relevance of doctrine to the individual (as he or she attempts to make sense of personal experience), the following chapter is especially concerned with the relevance of doctrine to the Christian church. Doctrine shapes corporate identity.

5 BELIEVING AND BELONGING: DOCTRINE AND CHRISTIAN IDENTITY

Doctrine is there to help the church to be what it is called to be. It shapes the vision of the world associated with the body of Christ. It could be said that doctrine gives Christians a sense of identity, at both the personal and the communal level. It explains what Christianity is all about. But this suggestion is open to a misunderstanding – that doctrine somehow invents a corporate identity. In fact, the Christian church has already been given its identity by the God who called it into being. The Christian church did not come into being of its own accord. It is a response to the calling of God. The initiative lies with God, who has called the church out (the root meaning of the Greek word *ekklesia*) of the world – called it out of darkness into his wonderful light.

JESUS CHRIST AND CHRISTIAN IDENTITY

In calling the church out of the world through the life, death and resurrection of Jesus Christ, God has given the church its identity. Its reason for existence is the proclamation of Jesus Christ, which is seen to be charged with the potential to transform the world, to bring about a new creation. Christians, as a body and as individuals, are called to affirm the judgement of the world in Christ. They witness to the new creation which lies on the other side of this judgement. A new life and a new lifestyle result from faith in the death and resurrection of Jesus Christ. God interrupts our lives and offers to change them through the transforming presence and power of Christ.

The fundamental reason for the church being there is thus Jesus Christ. At first sight, this may seem an astonishingly naive and blinkered statement. Surely the church is there to bring about fair social conditions? Surely Christians are called to transform society, to bring about a new and more just world? Yet, on reflection, the wisdom of the statement becomes clear. Christian values – the values which must govern our understanding of what 'justice' means – arise in the wake of Jesus Christ. As John Rawls stressed in his *Theory of Justice*, there is little to be gained from asserting the need for justice, unless it can be given some shape and specification. It needs to be earthed, unless it is to remain an abstract and unusable concept. The Christian cannot simply baptise secular ideas of justice. Many such ideas of justice rest upon profoundly unchristian ideas about the nature and destiny of humanity. Ideas of justice reflect world-views and values. The pressure for the Christian to transform the world is the result of our vision of what God wishes his world to be like, a vision of the new creation in Christ. To insist that Christianity centres on Jesus Christ is to declare that, in him and through him, we have access to ideas and values which govern the Christian vision of how the world should be.

Doctrine thus seeks to preserve the identity of the church. It enables the Christian church to remain faithful to its calling, and to the one who called it into being. It does this partly in a negative way, by declaring that Christians cannot simply baptise secular ideas of justice, integrity and morality. It is unquestionably much easier for Christians to accept secular views of justice, such as those developed until recently with vigour and conviction by Marxist social analysts. It is much easier to gain a hearing by endorsing existing secular political attitudes. Yet these views and attitudes rest upon theories of the nature and destiny of human beings which generally profoundly contradict those of the Christian faith. Marxist values rest upon Marxist doctrines, such as the non-existence of God and the inevitability of socialism – just as Christian values ultimately rest upon Christian doctrines. A failure to realise the extent to which values, attitudes and actions rest upon *doctrinal* foundations explains much of the moral shallowness of Christian liberalism in recent years.

The belief which appears to underlie this liberalism – that all cultural values and attitudes are somehow 'God-given', and thus to be respected – is alarmingly naive. It ignores, for example, the significant extent to which they are shaped and manipulated by powerful groups within society for their own ends. Culture can be little more than successful politics. Sexual domination, racial exclusivism, the perpetuation of the dominance of one social grouping over another on religious grounds (one of the most crippling aspects of the Hindu caste system), the belief that profits justify exploitation of individuals – all are examples of profoundly unchristian cultural attitudes which have been created and moulded by power groups, eager to preserve their own privileged positions. Doctrine passes judgement on these attitudes by destroying the delusions about human nature and destiny, and about the nature and purposes of God himself, upon which they are ultimately based.

Doctrine also serves a positive function. It affirms what is distinctive about Christianity. It identifies what is unique, what is identity-giving, about the gospel. It criticises the church and individual believers when they lapse into vague generalities about the gospel, or lose sight of its uniqueness and God-given relevance to the world. It affirms that God has called the Christian church into existence for a reason.

Doctrine presupposes the existence of the church – not a doctrine of the church, but a historical community of faith which confesses Jesus Christ as Lord. The common life of prayer, reading of Scripture and worship, of this community, provides the stimulus for doctrinal reflection. Doctrine arises within the community of faith, as it seeks to make sense and give order and structure to its experience of and encounter with God through the risen Christ. Doctrine is thus an 'insider' phenomenon, reflecting the hopes and beliefs of the Christian community of faith – above all, its experience of forgiveness and new life through Christ. Outside this context, doctrine may seem barren and lifeless. It may seem little more than a collection of hair-splitting distinctions. But what needs to be explained to such people is not specific *doctrines*, but what doctrine attempts to represent – the redemptive communal experience of the risen Christ as Lord. What moves Christians to make doctrinal statements is the wish and need to give substance and expression to their experience of God in Christ. The impulse which animates the genesis of doctrine is thus prior to any specific doctrinal formulations as such – yet, paradoxically, requires precisely some such doctrinal formulation if it is to be transmitted from one generation to another.

This allows us to make an important distinction between 'doctrine' and 'theology'. 'Doctrine' implies a reference to the ideas of a community, whose members value and are committed to them. 'Theology' more properly refers to the views of individuals, not necessarily within this community or tradition, who seek to explore ideas without any necessary commitment to them. Doctrine possesses a strongly representative character, attempting to describe or prescribe the beliefs of a community. Of course, Christian communities include some theologians within them – but those theologians do not speak *on behalf of* that community. The community is not committed to the ideas of its theologians. The community is at liberty to appropriate or reject their speculation. Doctrine entails a sense of *commitment* to a community, and a sense of *obligation* to speak on its behalf, where the corporate mind of the community exercises a restraint over the individual's perception of truth. Doctrine is an *activity*, a process of transmission of the collective wisdom of a community concerning its experience of Jesus Christ. The views of theologians can be doctrinally significant – if they have won acceptance within the community (a process generally referred to as 'reception'). The concept of 'reception' is of central importance to the concept of doctrine, in that a community is involved in the assessment of whether a decision, judgement or theological opinion is consistent with their corporate understanding of the Christian faith. Doctrine is communally authoritative teachings regarded as essential to the identity of the Christian community.

DOCTRINE AND CHRISTIAN IDENTITY

We can now begin to explore the theme of 'doctrine and Christian identity' in more detail. Two basic principles govern this vital aspect of Christian doctrine.

1. Doctrine distinguishes the Christian church from the world, including non-Christian religions and western secular culture.
2. Doctrine distinguishes one Christian denomination from another.

The recent rise of the New Age movement has highlighted the crucial importance of doctrine in the modern western world. For doctrine allows one religious group to be distinguished from another – including the New Age movement from orthodox Christianity. Occasionally, religious groups seem to be very similar to each other – yet, on closer inspection, they prove to have radically different ideas about such crucial matters as the character and purposes of God, and human nature and destiny. To understand this crucial aspect of Christian doctrine further, let us consider four different situations in the history of the Christian church.

1. The Early Church

Initially, Christianity had to define itself over and against Judaism. After all, Christianity emerged from within Judaism, yet regarded itself as distinct from it. So how could continuity with the great Old Testament tradition be affirmed, while at the same time making clear that Christianity was not Jewish? Paul's doctrine of justification by faith is an excellent example of a doctrine which, on the one hand, *affirms* the continuity between the Old and New Testaments, and on the other, *distinguishes* Christianity from Judaism. The doctrine affirms that the great promises made by God to Abraham and his successors now apply to Christian believers – without in any way implying that they required to be circumcised, or observe the Jewish law, as a result.

As Christianity expanded into the Mediterranean world of the second century, however, the question of its relation to Judaism became increasingly distant and irrelevant. Christianity now had to define itself over and against a number of key movements in the world of this period. One of these movements was Gnosticism. The central problem with Gnosticism was that, in many respects, it seemed virtually identical to Christianity. Gnostic beliefs (which, incidentally, bear more than a passing resemblance to those of modern New Age movements) seemed very close to those of Christianity. Gnostic writers appealed to Christians to join them, arguing that they basically believed the same things.

This precipitated a crisis of identity within Christianity during the second century. It became increasingly obvious that Christian groups would have to pay much more attention to thinking through what they believed. It meant that thought had to be given to developing criteria by which the claims of groups to be 'Christian churches' could be tested. Gnosticism posed a powerful challenge to the Christian church, in effect forcing the latter to clarify its boundaries. The Gnostics argued that they had received a secret tradition, directly from the apostles, to which Christians did not have access. They had access to secret saving knowledge (the word 'Gnostic' comes from the Greek word *gnosis*, 'knowledge'). The Christian church vigorously denied this, arguing that everything necessary for salvation was openly available through Scripture. Yardsticks – such as the canon of the New Testament, or adherence to the apostolic rule of faith, summed up in the Apostles' Creed – were agreed by which the claims of religious communities to be Christian churches could be checked out.

One of the most important Christian writers to deal with this emerging problem was Irenaeus (c.130–c.200), a bishop in the southern Gallic city of Lyons. Irenaeus insisted that the basic elements of the Christian faith were public knowledge, and not some secret tradition available only to the few. He drew up a number of short statements of faith, which summarised the basic Christian teaching on certain key subjects. Christians believe

in one God, the maker of heaven and earth, and of all the things that are in them, through Jesus Christ the Son of God, who, on account of his overwhelming love for his creation, endured the birth from the Virgin, uniting man to God in himself, and suffered under Pontius Pilate, and rose again, and was taken up in majesty, and will come again in glory, the saviour of those who are saved and the judge of those who are judged.

This statement (which is basically a prototype of the Apostles' Creed) served to distinguish Christians from non-Christians, such as Gnostics. It created a sense of identity among the Christian churches, which were often geographically isolated in the far-flung Roman Empire. All Christian communities and believers, Irenaeus stressed, shared the same faith. Although the church was scattered from one end of the earth to the other, it shared common doctrines deriving directly from the apostles through Scripture.

Doctrinal formulations began to become particularly important in this way towards the end of the second century. Nevertheless, this does not appear to have been understood as an attempt primarily to define what individual Christians believed; rather, it seems to have been intended as a means by which the credentials of a community or movement claiming to be a Christian church might be tested. To allow Christianity to be confused with Gnosticism would result in the gospel becoming diluted and confused, losing sight of many central insights of the New Testament.

2. Medieval Christendom

With the conversion of the Roman emperor Constantine (AD 312), a new situation began to develop. Under the Edict of Milan (AD 313), Christianity assumed a new status as the official religion of the Roman Empire, eventually leading to the development of medieval 'Christendom'. The Roman Empire was officially Christian, and there was thus no longer any need to distinguish Christians from their neighbours. With this development, doctrine lost its identity-giving function. 'Church' and 'society' were regarded as more or less the same thing. Doctrine was no longer of importance, in that Christianity no longer felt any need to distinguish itself from society. Society, it was argued, *was* Christian.

This is not to say, of course, that the medieval church had no interest in doctrine whatsoever. It is simply to note that doctrine was not seen as a criterion of identity in the period, except in the specific area of combatting heresy. 'Christendom' was sufficiently stable and well-defined to allow the need for doctrinal self-definition to become of little relevance. It is precisely this lack of interest in doctrine which is widely held to underlie the origins of the Reformation: doctrinal confusion and vagueness on certain key issues (such as justification by faith) in the first two decades of the sixteenth century led Luther to feel that the church of his day had lost sight of the true gospel. Medieval European

Christendom, through losing interest in doctrine, had also lost touch with the gospel.

3. The German Reformation

With the advent of the Reformation, however, the situation changed significantly. Martin Luther's programme of reform at Wittenberg in the late 1510s and early 1520s centred on a specific doctrine – justification by faith alone. It was on the basis of this doctrine that Luther and his colleagues, eventually to become the Lutheran church, would take their stand against the papacy and the world. Germany became the arena of confrontation between two rival groups – Lutheranism and Roman Catholicism – each claiming to be authentically Christian. They had to distinguish themselves from one another. And the easiest and most reliable way of distinguishing themselves was through doctrine.

The Roman Catholic church responded to Lutheranism at the Council of Trent, which defined Catholic ideas on doctrines such as justification with unprecedented clarity. Trent provided a remarkably comprehensive statement of Catholic doctrine, thus providing an explicit definition of the boundaries of the Roman Catholic church. The Reformation thus restored the identity-giving function of Christian doctrine.

The situation in Germany became even more complicated during the 1560s and 1570s, as Calvinism began to make major inroads into previously Lutheran territory. Three major Christian denominations were now firmly established in the same area – Lutheranism, Calvinism, and Roman Catholicism. All three were under major pressure to *identify* themselves. Lutherans were obliged to explain how they differed from Calvinists on the one hand, and Roman Catholics on the other. And doctrine proved the most reliable way of identifying and explaining these differences: 'We believe this, but they believe that.' The period 1559–1622, characterised by its new emphasis upon doctrine, is generally referred to as the 'Period of Orthodoxy'.

Lutheranism and Calvinism were, in many respects, very similar. Thus both claimed to be evangelical, and rejected more or less the same central aspects of medieval Catholicism. But they needed to be distinguished. And doctrine proved to be the most reliable way of distinguishing two otherwise very similar bodies. At most points of doctrine, Lutherans and Calvinists were in broad agreement. Yet there was one matter – the doctrine of predestination – upon which they were radically divided. (Lutherans held that predestination referred to God's general decision that anyone who came to faith would be saved; Calvinists argued that it referred to his specific decisions concerning which individuals would be saved.) The emphasis placed upon the doctrine of predestination by Calvinists in the period 1559–1662 partly reflects the fact that this doctrine distinguished them from their Lutheran colleagues.

4. The English Reformation

The sixteenth-century English Reformation under Henry VIII bore little relation to its German equivalent. The historian F.W. Powicke remarked that 'the one thing that can be said about the Reformation in England is that it was an act of State . . . the Reformation in England was a parliamentary transaction.' There is enough truth in Powicke's generalisation to draw attention to a key difference between the German and English Reformations. In Germany, there was a protracted struggle between Lutheran and Roman Catholic, as each attempted to gain influence in a disputed region. In England, Henry VIII simply declared that there would only be one national church within his realm. By royal command, there would only be one Christian body within England. The reformed English church was under no pressure to define itself in relation to any other Christian body in the region. The manner in which the English Reformation initially proceeded demanded no doctrinal self-definition, in that the church in England was defined *socially* in precisely

the same way before the Reformation as after, whatever
political alterations may have been introduced. This is not
to say that no theological debates took place in England at
the time of the Reformation; it is to note that they were
not seen as being of decisive importance. They were not
regarded as identity-giving.

The Lutheran church in Germany was obliged to define
and defend its existence and boundaries by doctrine because
it had broken away from the medieval Catholic church.
That church continued to exist around Lutheran regions,
forcing Lutheranism to carry on justifying its existence. The
Henrician church in England, however, regarded itself as
continuous with the medieval church. The English church
was sufficiently well defined as a social unit to require no
further definition at the doctrinal level.

The situation remained much the same under Elizabeth
I. The 'Elizabethan Settlement' (1559) laid down that there
would only be one Christian church in England – the
Church of England, which retained the monopoly of the
pre-Reformation church, while replacing it with a church
which recognised royal, rather than papal, authority. The
phrase 'Church of England', as defined legally in Halsbury's
Laws of England, makes no reference to its doctrine: the
'Church of England' is regarded as continuous with the
church established in England during the period 597–686.
Roman Catholicism, Lutheranism and Calvinism – the
three Christian churches fighting it out for dominance
of the continent of Europe – would not be tolerated
within England. There was thus no particular reason for
the Church of England to bother much about doctrinal
questions. Elizabeth ensured that it had no rivals within
England. One of the purposes of doctrine is to divide –
and there was nothing for the Church of England to divide
itself from. England was insulated from the factors which
made doctrine so significant a matter on the mainland of
Europe in the Reformation and immediate post-Reformation
periods.

Indeed, the need to ensure that all English Christians (whether inclined towards some form of Protestantism or Roman Catholicism) felt reasonably at home in the Church of England led to the importance of doctrine being played down: an emphasis on doctrine might lead to divisions within the new church, and hence to internal weakness. As Elizabeth tried to ensure England's safety in the dangerous world of the late sixteenth century, the last thing she wanted was an England torn apart by doctrinal differences. A divided English church would be a divided England; and a divided England would be a weak England, vulnerable to foreign subversion or invasion from France or Spain.

That situation, however, has now changed completely. Today, the Church of England is no longer the only significant Christian body in England, on account of the growth of evangelicalism, the rapid expansion of the house church movement, and the new confidence evident within English Roman Catholicism; the notion of the 'establishment' of the Church of England has degenerated into little more than a legal fiction. English society as a whole is now not merely non-Christian (due, amongst other factors, to the extensive immigration of Moslems and Hindus from the Indian subcontinent), but is even at points aggressively secularist. In addition, there is a new threat from religious groups which – like Gnosticism in the early church period – bear a superficial resemblance to Christianity, yet are actually profoundly unchristian. The New Age movement is a case in point. There is thus a growing need for self-definition on the part of the Church of England, if it is to survive as a distinctive Christian body – and an inevitable part of that process of self-identification is a new attention to matters of doctrine. We argued above that the traditional marginalisation of doctrine within the Church of England partly reflects the specific social, religious and political situation of sixteenth-century England, now radically altered through a process of historical erosion. A new social situation demands a new – and more positive – attitude to doctrine. The twentieth century cannot be fettered with obsolete hangovers of the sixteenth century. The new interest in doctrinal matters evident among younger English Anglicans reflects this point, and echoes a wider recognition of the importance of doctrine within many other churches.

A HIERARCHY OF DOCTRINES

Doctrine, as we have seen, divides Christianity from the world, giving Christian denominations a unity over and against secular culture and other religions; it also, however, divides denominations from one another. There is thus a tension in the function of doctrine. On the one hand, it unites Christians against non-Christians; on the other, it divides one Christian from another. Once this fact has been recognised, an important conclusion may be drawn: not all Christian doctrines are of equal importance. This insight has been explained and justified using two different, though related, models – that of a hierarchy on the one hand, and a concentric series of circles on the other. We shall explore both.

Christianity possesses a hierarchy of doctrines. By this is meant the following. Doctrines are not all of equal importance. At the top of the hierarchy is a cluster of fundamental doctrines, the denial of which involves setting oneself outside the Christian church. Beneath this cluster of doctrines are to be found a group of non-essential doctrines, of varying degrees of importance. While all Christians are (or ought to be) united on the fundamentals of faith, disagreement is to be accepted on secondary matters.

In the sixteenth century the German Lutheran writer Philip Melanchthon introduced a new word into the vocabulary of theologians. The word Melanchthon coined is *adiaphora* – 'matters of indifference'. For Melanchthon, the gospel consists of a central core, centering upon the gracious redemption of sinners in Jesus Christ. This central core is surrounded by a concentric ring, containing doctrines of secondary importance. Disagreement upon these matters among Christians might be tolerated, provided the doctrines in the central core region were not called into question or denied. To affirm the doctrines in the core region is to be a Christian; to affirm the doctrines in the outer circle is to be a particular kind of Christian.

Both these models raise the same question: what are the fundamentals, and what are the secondary doctrines, or 'matters of indifference'? Modern ecumenical discussions have centred upon identifying which doctrines are essential to Christian belief, and which are open to debate. On the basis of these discussions, some illustrations of each type of doctrine could be given.

Fundamental doctrines, essential to Christian identity
- the divinity of Jesus Christ
- the humanity of Jesus Christ
- the existence of God
- the doctrine of salvation by grace through faith
- the divinity of the Holy Spirit
- the Trinity

Secondary doctrines, upon which disagreement may be permitted within Christianity
- whether, and in what way, Christ is present in the sacraments
- whether baptism signifies or causes believers to be born again
- whether 'justification' means 'declaring righteous' or 'making righteous' (or something in between?)
- in what precise way Jesus is both God and man

Thus, on the basis of this analysis, Christians ought to be united on the fact that Jesus is both God and man, but at liberty to disagree on the most appropriate way of making sense of this mystery. In other words it is the fact, rather than any particular theory, of the incarnation which is fundamental to the Christian faith. Doctrine thus attempts to define what is essential and fundamental to Christianity, while at the same time mapping out areas in which debate is possible. It encourages Christians throughout the world and across doctrinal divisions to value and affirm the fundamentals which they have in common, rather than dwelling upon the differences which divide them. It affirms the common identity and purpose of Christians, to enable them to be faithful to their calling in the world.

This process of reflection has been encouraged by the rise of the ecumenical movement, probably one of the most important developments in modern Christian history. There is a new willingness on the part of many denominations to build bridges, and to attempt to overcome the division of the churches. A central feature of this process of drawing together is engagement with doctrinal matters. The heritage of doctrinal disagreements between denominations has been subjected to critical examination concerning its biblical foundations, and its originating historical circumstances. This has helped to identify on the one hand a common core of central and essential Christian doctrines, shared by all Christian believers, and on the other hand, a number of areas in which genuine disagreement may be accepted.

For many Christians, these divisions are painful. It hurts when Christians disagree amongst themselves. Why should the church be disunited in this way? Why can't Christians be agreed upon everything? If you feel like this, remember that all Christians share a central core of faith. What they have in common far outweighs their differences. It is natural to concentrate upon differences, and forget how much Christians have in common with one another. Yet it is far more important that a person should know the risen Christ, than that they should express their faith in him in some particular way. Forms of words, ways of expression, and patterns of worship vary between Christians in one part of the world and another – but underlying them all is the same Lord. So learn to be positive, and concentrate upon what Christians have in common, over and against the world.

Doctrine, then, is there to help the church become what it has been called to be. It achieves this goal, in part, in a defensive manner. An illustration may help to summarise this crucial function of doctrine. Consider a medieval English castle, with an inner keep and outer defensive fortifications, such as a wall and a moat. The real hub of the castle is the keep. The life of the castle centres upon it. The walls and other fortifications are there merely to defend the keep in times of danger. So it is with doctrine. The real life-blood of the Christian faith is not doctrines as such, but the real and transforming presence of Jesus Christ in the life of individuals and the church. Doctrines are there to defend that presence.

In times of peace, the castle walls could be allowed to fall into a certain amount of disrepair. There was no need for them to be permanently manned. No threat was posed to the keep. In the Middle Ages, there was no particular need for any emphasis upon doctrine – no real threat existed to the Christian faith. But that situation changed. The moment a dangerous situation developed, the castle walls had to be repaired. They were manned constantly, in order to defend the keep against new threats. And so the church must be prepared to rediscover the importance of doctrine, where the Christian gospel is under threat. It is under threat in the western world, not least because of the new and aggressively secular attitudes of western society. Other factors underscore the need for Christianity to rediscover its identity, and state it in doctrinal terms – for example, the rise of militant Islam world-wide, and the birth of the New Age movement. Doctrine matters more now than it has mattered for a long time.

Doctrine thus aims to keep the church faithful to the God who has called it into being, and to the proclamation of the good news of Jesus Christ. It summons the church to a contemplative and obedient receptivity to the challenge and judgement of Jesus Christ. We must be prepared to yield to this challenge and judgement, in that Christian identity is not determined by human agents, but by the God who called the Christian church into being, and defined its tasks. This is no call to a blind obedience to authority, but a faithful and obedient response to truth. Doctrine is no intellectual strait-jacket, imposed to silence discussion within the church. Rather, it is the outcome of a loving and committed process of reflection on the central symbol of the Christian faith – the cross of Christ. Here lies the true identity of the Christian individual and the Christian community – and doctrine is an attempt to spell out that identity, in order that it may be preserved in the present and transmitted to the future. It is an attempt – a bold and necessary attempt – to keep the 'salt of the earth' salty. For if that salt 'loses its saltiness, how can it be made salty again? It is no longer good for anything, except to be thrown out and trampled' (Matt. 5:13).

In the last four chapters, we have been considering what doctrine is. It will be clear that doctrine serves a number of vital purposes. The second part of this work consolidates these impressions, by explaining in more detail why doctrine is of such importance to the Christian church.

Part II

Doctrine: Why it matters

6 DOCTRINE AND FAITH

Christianity is about coming to life in all its fullness. One of the reasons why Christianity has been so powerful a force in world history for so long is that it possesses the ability to change human lives. This ability is not some sort of add-on extra, an option or extension which can be added to the basic package. It is fundamental to the nature of the Christian gospel itself. Let three twentieth-century people relate how this happened to them.

I had been running away from God for a long time. I just knew he was there. And then I came home to him. I just gave up running away from him, and asked him to come into my life. I knew he was real, and I knew he wanted me. I've never looked back on that moment.

You must picture me alone in that room at Magdalen, night after night, feeling, whenever my mind lifted even for a second from my work, the steady unrelenting approach of Him whom I so earnestly desired not to meet. That which I greatly feared had at last come upon me. In the Trinity Term of 1929 I gave in, and admitted that God was God, and knelt and prayed: perhaps, that night, the most dejected and reluctant convert in all England.

There might be no certainty that Christ was God – but, by God, there was no certainty that he was not. This was not to be borne. I could not reject Jesus. There was only one thing to do once I had seen the gap behind me. I turned away from it, and flung myself over the gap towards Jesus.

These three people – an Oxford student, C.S. Lewis, and the American writer Sheldon Vanauken – are describing how they came to faith. The pattern is slightly different in each case. They express themselves in different ways. Yet there is a common core to them. Each discovered the reality of God. Countless others could tell similar stories of how they made that same discovery.

'Now that's what Christianity is *really* about!' some may say. 'It's got nothing to do with doctrinal nit-picking and hair-splitting. It's about making a personal discovery of God. It's about wanting to serve him in the world. It's about praising and adoring him. How on earth can something so real, something so pulsating with life, have anything to do with the drab and dreary statements of the creed or doctrine textbooks? We can do without those very well.'

This is a powerful criticism. It reflects the feeling of some, especially those who have had a dramatic conversion experience, that the reality of God is somehow compromised by doctrinal statements. God is real; doctrines, however, often seem abstract and unreal. Take 'justification by faith'. Most people don't understand what this doctrine means, let alone what its relevance might be. The words are strange; the idea seems unintelligible. Doctrines often create a bad impression on outsiders, who come to think of Christianity as little more than a list of things you have to believe. The creeds often seem like little more than checklists of beliefs. And a serious misunderstanding of Christianity can come about as a result – the idea that Christian faith is just accepting certain things as true. But it is through exploring the nature of faith that we can begin to gain a preliminary understanding of why doctrine is of such central importance to the Christian believer and the Christian church.

THE NATURE OF FAITH

Faith, in the full-blooded Christian sense of the word, is a complex notion, bringing together a cluster of key ideas. Its basic sense, as found in the New Testament, could be summarised as 'the new way of existence made possible through the death and resurrection of Jesus Christ'. The English word 'belief' is, unfortunately, quite incapable of bringing out the full meaning of the New Testament concept of faith. It seems to suggest that the life, death and resurrection of Jesus changes our ideas – but not our lives. The New Testament word for faith, *pistis*, seems to embrace all of the following ideas.

1. Faith as assent

Faith believes that certain things are true. 'I believe in God' means something like 'I believe that there is a God,' or 'I think that God exists.' Faith assents belief in the existence of God. This is an essential starting point. After all, before we can begin to say anything about what God is like, we need to assume that there is a God in the first place. It is interesting to note that many people outside the Christian faith have the impression that there is nothing more to Christian faith than assent to God's existence. Christian belief is little more than running through a checklist of propositions – such as those contained in the creeds. That is why it is essential to realise that Christian faith, for the New Testament writers, includes the idea of trust.

2. Faith as trust

When I declare that 'I believe in God', I am not just saying that I believe that God exists. I am affirming my trust in him. Faith cannot be equated with knowing. It is not something purely intellectual, enlightening the mind while leaving the heart untouched. Faith is the response of our whole person to the person of God. It is a joyful reaction on our part to the overwhelming divine love we see revealed in Jesus Christ. It is the simple response of leaving all to follow Jesus. Faith is both our recognition that something wonderful has happened through the life, death and resurrection of Jesus Christ, and our response to what has happened. Faith realises that God loves us, and responds to that love. Faith is saying 'Yes' to God.

Christians don't just *believe* – we believe *in someone*. Faith is like an anchor, linking us with the object of faith. Just as an anchor secures a ship to the ocean floor, so our faith links us securely with God. Faith is not just believing that God exists; it is about anchoring ourselves to that God, and resting secure in doing so. Whatever storms life may bring, the anchor of faith will hold us firm to God.

Perhaps the clearest exposition of this aspect of faith may be found in Hebrews 11:1–12:3. This famous passage opens with a definition of faith (11:1) as 'being sure of what we hope for and certain of what we do not see.' What this means is illustrated by the trust of the individuals mentioned in the remainder of the chapter. Abraham was called to go to a strange land to receive his inheritance (11:8) – and he trusted God, and went. All believed that God could be trusted, and acted on the basis of that faith. This great passage closes (12:1–3) by urging us to consider all these great men and women of faith, to learn from their example, and to trust God as they did.

The story is told of the great French tightrope walker Blondin, who crossed the Niagara Falls on a tightrope. One of the American onlookers congratulated him on his achievement. 'Do you believe I could do it again?' the Frenchman asked him. 'Certainly!' came the unhesitant reply. 'Well, why don't you let me carry you across?' Blondin replied. The American blushed, and hastily melted into the waiting crowd. He might have been prepared to believe that something could be done – but he wasn't prepared to put himself at risk on the basis of his belief. Many individuals believe that God exists, and that he is able to forgive the sins of those who trust in him – but are not prepared actually to take that step of faith. That is why commitment is so important an element of Christian faith.

3. Faith as commitment

Time and time again, Scripture encourages us to think of our faith as a personal relationship with God. God is one who has publicly demonstrated his commitment to and love for us in the cross of Jesus Christ; he will not abandon us. He will be with us, wherever we go. Faith is our commitment to God, our decision to allow him to be present with us, to guide us, to support us, to challenge us and to rule us. It is a joyful and willing self-surrender to God. It is a throwing open of the doors of our lives, and inviting God to enter, not merely as our guest, but as our Lord and master. God's commitment to us demands a commitment from us in return. Just as God humbled himself on the cross to meet us, so we must humble ourselves in repentance to meet him.

It is helpful to remember the close links between the creed and baptism in the early church. When Christian converts declared that they believed in God, in Jesus Christ, and in the Holy Spirit, they were declaring publicly their commitment to the gospel. They were not just telling the world *what* they believed about Jesus Christ; they were telling the world *that* they believed in Jesus Christ. At the time, this was a risky business: to admit to being a Christian was to open yourself to ridicule, discrimination, victimisation and possibly much worse. To 'come out' as a Christian was a matter of real courage. 'I believe in God' means 'I have committed myself to God.' To believe in God is to belong to God. It is also to obey God.

Writing to the Christians at Rome, Paul mentions 'the obedience that comes from faith' (Rom. 1:5). At one point, he gives thanks to God that the faith of the Roman Christians is being reported all over the world (Rom. 1:8); at another, that their obedience is being reported everywhere (Rom. 16:19). Faith, then, leads to obedience. It is a willingness to trust and obey the God who has called us to faith in him. We are called to be doers, rather than just hearers of the Word of God (Jas. 1:22; 2:14–20).

These elements of trust and commitment are of central importance to the Christian understanding of faith. Suppose you are on a walking holiday by the coast. As you walk along the shoreline one day, you notice a small island a short distance from land. The receding tide has uncovered a sand causeway leading to the island. Intrigued, you walk out, and begin to explore it. The first object you notice is a small rowing boat, moored to a rock. As you clamber over the rocks of the island, your attention is drawn to the richness of its animal and plant life. The receding tide has left behind countless rock pools, filled with sea life of every kind. This brings out the amateur marine biologist in you, and you spend hours happily identifying types of molluscs.

When you next look up, you realise that the tide has begun to come in. The sand causeway is already submerged. A thought flashes through your mind. 'If things get really dangerous, that boat would be a way of escape.' As you clamber down the rocks to the waterline, you discover that the tide has already reached a dangerously high level, and that it would be impossible to wade back to the shore. You scan the shoreline in desperation, hoping that there is someone within earshot who might be able to help you. But you are utterly alone. As the tide rises further, you remember that an exceptionally high tide is due today. There is every chance that you will be swept away by its current. Your only hope of escape lies with the boat. You jump in, cast off, and row for the safety of the shore.

In the course of this adventure, your attitude to the boat passes through three quite different stages. Initially, you see the boat as little more than a feature of the landscape. It exists. It is there. But it has no particular relevance to your situation. You are perfectly prepared to affirm that it exists – but whether it exists or not is of little importance. As you become aware of the danger of your situation, however, a new attitude to the boat emerges: it is a potential means of escape. It is seen as a way in which you – or anyone else in the same situation – could escape from danger. You may not yet have reached the stage where you want to make use of it. You might want to explore other ways of getting out of this jam. But you are prepared to believe that the boat could be a way out. And finally, you come to the point where you decide to trust the boat. Your faith expresses itself in action and commitment, as you get into it, and put to sea.

The same three stages can be seen with attitudes to God. First, there is the attitude which is prepared to admit that he exists. The statement 'There is a God' is accepted intellectually. The second stage involves accepting that God could be of some relevance to anyone who was in trouble. This still lacks personal application, however: God may be of relevance and importance to someone else – but not (yet) to me. Finally, there is the stage at which God becomes important at a personal level. He is of direct relevance to *me*. A new element enters into the equation – that of trust and personal commitment.

THE IMPORTANCE OF DOCTRINE: CAN WE TRUST GOD?

All the words used in the previous section – trust, commitment and obedience – need qualification. Who or what do we trust? Why do we trust them? Who do we commit ourselves to? Who do we obey? Christian faith is not blind obedience. If people demand that we obey them, we naturally want to know why. What is it about them that gives them the authority to demand our obedience? If people demand that we trust them, we have every right to ask whether they are worthy of that trust. Why should I put my trust in

Jesus Christ? Why should anyone base his or her entire life upon him? Earlier, we quoted Sheldon Vanauken's words concerning his leap of faith: 'I could not reject Jesus. There was only one thing to do once I had seen the gap behind me. I turned away from it, and flung myself over the gap towards Jesus.' Vanauken here describes making a leap of faith, as he committed himself to Jesus Christ. But why? What grounds did he have for making this commitment? As many Germans discovered to their horror in the 1930s, it is perfectly possible to put your trust in someone who, like Adolf Hitler, eventually turns out to be something approaching the devil incarnate. It is equally possible to commit yourself to someone or something profoundly evil and destructive, as the story of Dr Faust's pact with the devil brings out. It is perfectly possible to believe in the authority and reliability of something which, like the Book of Mormon, turns out to be a crude forgery, a human invention. In all these cases, faith is shattered by reality; such a faith can only survive by blindly, doggedly and obstinately ignoring the truth. How could Vanauken be reasonably sure that his faith would not be shattered like this? How could he know he was not flinging himself into an abyss, a bottomless pit, an empty void?

This point is brought out clearly by Francis Schaeffer, in his much-admired book *He Is There and He Is Not Silent*. Schaeffer suggests that we imagine a group of mountaineers, high up in the Swiss Alps. As they scale the bare rock, they are suddenly engulfed by fog. Their position becomes dangerous, as ice begins to form. One of the climbers suggests that they take a 'leap of faith' – letting go of their hold on the rock, in the hope that they will land safely on an unseen ledge some short distance below. There is, however, no evidence that such a ledge exists. None of them knows the area, or has any idea what lies beneath them. To trust in their colleague's advice would be a blind leap of faith, a shot in the dark. The mountaineers would be fools if they trusted him blindly in this manner.

Then, Schaeffer continues, the climbers hear a voice calling to them through the fog. The unseen speaker tells the climbers that he is an experienced guide, a veteran mountaineer who knows the area like the back of his hand. He tells them that, although they cannot see it, there is indeed a place of safety just below them. By letting go of the rock, they will save themselves. The mountaineers are in a position to challenge the reliability, competence and truthfulness of the speaker. They are not being asked to trust blindly in his judgement. They are being invited to verify the trustworthiness of the speaker before obeying him. They have the opportunity to know something about him before committing themselves to him.

It is this vital need to know *about* God which underlies the importance of Christian doctrine. Doctrine is concerned with defending and explaining the utter trustworthiness, integrity and truthfulness of God, as we know him in Scripture and through Jesus Christ. It is vital that Christians rest assured that the God in whom they have put their faith is profoundly worthy of that trust. One example will help to bring out this point. The doctrine of salvation through Christ assures us that God redeems us in a way in which his integrity and ours is preserved. We are not redeemed by exploiting some legal loophole, by ignoring our sin, or by compromising God's own righteousness.

Why did God have to redeem us through the death of Christ on the cross? Why couldn't he have done something much simpler? For example, why could he not have simply declared sin to be forgiven and forgotten? After all, God is merciful – why can't he just show that mercy by overlooking sin, or telling us that it doesn't matter? There are many things that can be said about God. For example, he is merciful; he is wise; he is righteous. All of these can be determined without any difficulty from Scripture. But these qualities, or attributes, of God cannot be considered in isolation from each other. God isn't merciful on Mondays and Tuesdays, wise on Wednesdays and Thursdays, and righteous on Fridays and Saturdays. He is all of these things, all of the time.

God's mercy and his justice are both involved in the redemption of humanity. God's tender mercy makes him want to redeem us in the first place; his justice determines the way in which he redeems us. Both mercy and justice are thus involved in redemption – but they are involved in different ways. God's mercy leads to the *decision* to redeem; God's justice leads to the particular *method* of redemption chosen. Neither God's mercy nor his justice are suspended – they are both in operation.

Now if God just declared that sin was forgiven, his mercy would indeed be satisfied – but what about his justice? God's implacable hostility to sin would be compromised. God would give the impression of having done some shady deal, by which his own principles were compromised. One of the more spectacular episodes in American politics of the late 1980s was President Reagan's arms deal with Iran. Ronald Reagan – perhaps the most popular president of the United States in recent years – constantly affirmed his total opposition to terrorism. Terrorists should be isolated. President Reagan regarded the Iranians as terrorists, holding American hostages against international law. They should be quarantined. Nobody should do any deals with them.

And then it turned out that President Reagan had authorised the sale of military equipment to Iran. The same man who had used all his moral authority to oppose dealing with Iran was seen to have compromised his own principles. He was being inconsistent. Some even suggested that he was being dishonest. His popularity slumped. A new word – 'Irangate', by analogy with the Watergate scandal which brought down President Richard Nixon – briefly entered the political vocabulary of American journalists. The moral of this incident is clear: if you condemn something, don't compromise your principles by doing that thing yourself!

You can see how this applies to God and the redemption of humanity. As Scripture makes abundantly clear, God is totally opposed to sin. He loves the sinner, certainly – but the sin, he detests. If God were to be seen to act in such a way as to condone sin, his integrity would be compromised. If God were to pretend that sin didn't really matter, the scriptural condemnations of sin would be seen to be hollow. If God can act in such a way as to tolerate sin, failing to condemn it, why should we not behave in the same way? It is not enough that God *is* just – he must be *seen* to act in a just manner. The redemption of the world thus becomes a test case. Will God act publicly in the righteous manner that his condemnations of sin suggest? Or will he continue to condemn sin, while doing some kind of deal with it behind our backs, along the lines of Ronald Reagan and Iran?

Now Ronald Reagan was able to explain his action in dealing with Iran along the following lines: there were American hostages held by groups sympathetic to Iran. By doing a deal with Iran, it would be possible to speed up the release of these hostages. The end thus justified the means. But, as the opinion polls soon made clear, the American public was not impressed. The end *and the means* both had to be consistent with moral principles. The redemption of the world is admirable, as an end or goal – but the means by which this is attained must be seen to be principled. God has publicly to demonstrate his justice, his determination to deal with sin firmly and fairly, in the way in which he redeems the world. The Christian doctrine of redemption affirms that God demonstrates total integrity and trustworthiness in this central aspect of his dealings with us. He – unlike President Reagan – may be trusted. Faith trusts in a God whom doctrine affirms to be worthy of trust, and whom doctrine declares may be known and encountered through Jesus Christ.

Having encountered God through Jesus Christ, the Christian life is begun. And, once more, doctrine plays a major role. It shapes Christian attitudes towards God and the world, as we shall see in the chapter which follows.

7 DOCTRINE AND THE CHRISTIAN LIFE

A common complaint about doctrine runs along the following lines. 'Doctrine is out-dated and irrelevant. What really matters is our attitudes to other people, and our morality. Doctrine doesn't matter.' Dorothy L. Sayers reacted as follows to this suggestion in a lecture of 1940:

> The one thing I am here to say to you is this: that it is worse than useless for Christians to talk about the importance of Christian morality, unless they are prepared to take their stand upon the fundamentals of Christian theology. It is a lie to say that dogma does not matter; it matters enormously. It is fatal to let people suppose that Christianity is only a mode of feeling; it is virtually necessary to insist that it is first and foremost a rational explanation of the universe. It is hopeless to offer Christianity as a vaguely idealistic aspiration or a simple aspiration of a simple and consoling kind; it is, on the contrary, a hard, tough, exacting and complex doctrine, steeped in a drastic and uncompromising realism.

Attitudes depend on doctrine. Granted that Christian attitudes – as expressed, for example, in morality – are of central importance, the fundamental importance of doctrine will be obvious. But how does doctrine affect attitudes? To explore this theme, we will consider two key areas of Christian life: spirituality and ethics.

CHRISTIAN SPIRITUALITY

'Spirituality' is a poorly defined word. Nevertheless, it refers to one of the richest aspects of the Christian faith – the way in which we lead a 'spiritual life'. 'Spirituality' is about ways of deepening our knowledge and love of God, of leading a more authentically *Christian* life. In part, spirituality concerns adopting right attitudes towards God and his creation. Once more, those attitudes are shaped and informed by doctrines. Two examples will illustrate this point.

1. The doctrine of justification by faith

Modern western society, especially in the United States of America, is very achievement-orientated. "You are what you make of yourself' is a key slogan of the enterprise culture. You have to lift yourself up by your own bootlaces. Many are deeply influenced by the secular values of success instilled into us by our families and peers. And these secular attitudes have important spiritual spin-offs. Many feel that they must *do* something or *achieve* something before God can love them. The gospel proclamation of the *unconditionality* of God's love for us can be difficult for such people to accept – because it so obviously contradicts the standards of western culture. Surely they must do something before God can accept them? Many are taught that dependency on others is to be discouraged. As a result, they believe strongly in the cult of independence: personal fulfilment is based on not being dependent on anyone or anything. The idea that God loves us, however, is an invitation to learn to depend on God. This clashes with the set of values we have absorbed from secular culture, which asserts that the way to get ahead in the world is through being independent.

The Christian doctrine of justification by faith mounts a powerful challenge to these attitudes. We are asked to believe that we have been accepted by God through Jesus Christ, despite being unacceptable. Our status before God is something given, not something earned. As Martin Luther – whose name is especially associated with this key doctrine – put it: 'Sinners are attractive because they are loved; they are not loved because they are attractive.' God's love for us is not dependent upon our achievements. We can never earn our salvation. We do not need to be high achievers to become Christians; it is God, not us, who achieves things. The tranquillity of faith – so powerful a theme of Luther's spirituality – rests upon recognising that God has done all that is necessary for our salvation in Jesus Christ, and has done it well. We are asked to accept what God has done for us in Jesus Christ, and act upon it.

Luther died in the early hours of Thursday, 17 February 1546. His last word was '*Ja* – Yes', muttered as he lay dying, in response to one of his friends, who asked if he was 'willing to persevere in the Christian faith and doctrine that you have preached'. Shortly after his death, his friends found a note lying on a table in the same house. It was Luther's final written statement. Its last six words read, '*Wir sind Bettler. Hoc est verum*' – 'We are beggars. This is true.' For Luther, Christians are spiritual beggars, incapable of achieving anything unaided, and dependent totally upon the generosity of a God who gives. The doctrine of justification by faith could be summed up in Luther's final six words. God gives; we receive – gladly and gratefully.

2. The doctrine of creation

Many people feel frightened and lonely in the world. They are overwhelmed by the thought of the immensity of the universe. The stars studded in the night sky seem to emphasise the brevity and unimportance of human life. After all, even the nearest of those stars are billions of miles away, and become further from us with each moment that passes. The light from them now reaching us may have begun its journey centuries ago, long before we were born. The light from the sun takes a mere eight minutes to reach us; that from one of the nearer stars (Betelgeuse, in the constellation of Orion) takes nearly two hundred years. Every year, astronomers report the discovery of new and more distant galaxies. It becomes increasingly clear that the universe is a vast and lonely place. We can very easily feel alienated from it.

The doctrine of creation defuses this sense of loneliness. It allows us to feel at home in the world. It reminds us that we, like the rest of creation, were fashioned by God (Pss. 19:1; 102:25). We are here because God wants us to be here. We are not alone, but are in the very presence of the God who made and owns everything. We are in the presence of a friend, who knows us and cares for us. Behind the apparently faceless universe lies a person. The stars in the night sky are then no longer symbols of despair, but of hope – the same God who made *them* also *made us* and cares for us (Ps. 8). They are even reminders of God's promises, and their fulfilment (Gen. 15:1–6). This central doctrine affirms that we are here because we are meant to be here, in the presence of the God who created us and redeemed us.

The doctrine also disarms the threat of astrology – a particular concern for the Israelites while in exile in Babylon, who seem to have felt intimidated by Babylonian astrology. The stars, the Babylonians suggested, had a secret and baleful power over human destiny. To realise that the stars have been created by God is to understand that they are under his authority. He has called them by name (Ps. 147:4). The stars are under the same constraints of createdness as everything else. They cannot exercise a sinister power over us. It was not merely Babylonian astrology which taught some form of astral fatalism; similar ideas can be discerned within the modern New Age movements. The doctrine of creation allows these ideas to be set to one side; all of creation is under the authority, whether acknowledged or not, of the one who created it – and who makes himself known to and available to us in Jesus Christ.

Doctrine does more than generate and inform Christian spiritual attitudes. It also allows crucial insights concerning the shape and pattern of the Christian life. The doctrine of prevenient grace illustrates this point particularly well.

3. The doctrine of prevenient grace

Many Christians, looking back on their lives, are aware that God appears to have been somehow guiding them towards conversion. The doctrine of prevenient grace addresses this feeling ('prevenient' means 'going ahead of', or 'going in advance'). The doctrine is firmly grounded in Scripture. For example, Paul was aware that, long before his conversion, God was somehow preparing him for his mission to the Gentiles (Rom. 1:1–3). The doctrine was given new importance by Augustine of Hippo in the late fourth century.

Augustine was born in modern-day Algeria on 13 November 354. His mother was a Christian, and very much wanted her son to share her faith. Augustine had, however, other ideas. While his mother was praying for him, he slipped on a boat leaving North Africa for Rome. The story of Augustine's subsequent conversion at Milan several years later is well known. In his autobiography (the *Confessions*), Augustine tells how in August 386 he sat under a fig tree in the garden of his house at Milan, and heard some children playing in a neighbouring garden. They were singing as they played, and the words they sang were, 'Take up and read! Take up and read!' Augustine rushed indoors, opened his New Testament at random, and read the verses which stood out from the page: 'Clothe yourselves with the Lord Jesus Christ, and do not think about how to gratify the desires of the sinful nature' (Rom. 13:14). He closed the book, and told his friends he had become a Christian. On his return to North Africa, Augustine would assume responsibilities which marked him out as one of the greatest Christian leaders and thinkers of all time.

But as Augustine looked back on the events leading up to his conversion, he could not help but notice that God had been preparing him for this great moment. Somehow, God had gone before him, and prepared him for the crucial step of confrontation and conversion. Two episodes which Augustine recalled from his time in Italy bring out this point.

On his arrival at Milan, Augustine discovered that the local Christian bishop had a reputation as a splendid orator. As Augustine himself had ambitions to become a public orator, he decided to find out whether the reputation was merited. Perhaps he could pick up some tips which might come in useful later. Each Sunday, he slipped into the cathedral and listened to the bishop preach. Initially, he took a purely professional interest in the sermons as pieces of splendid oratory. But gradually, their content began to take hold of him. He developed an interest in Christianity. 'I had yet to discover that it taught the truth,' he later remarked, 'but I did discover that it did not teach the things I had accused it of.'

Later, Augustine began to go through a spiritual crisis. He broke off his relationship with his mistress – a relationship which had lasted fifteen years, and had given every appearance of stability to his colleagues. He developed a sense of spiritual lostness. But how could he change his ways so late in life? Surely he was too set in his ways to change? In the midst of this crisis, God seemed to speak to him. Augustine had long been attracted to the writings of the author Marius Victorinus: he now discovered that this writer had become a Christian late in life. A visitor to Augustine's residence told him of how Victorinus had been converted by studying the Scriptures, and had insisted on going to church and making a public declaration of faith. The visitor relished the story as a superb piece of gossip; for Augustine, however, it seemed to be the voice of God addressing him in secret. If Marius Victorinus could do it, so could Augustine. Another fundamental psychological block to conversion had been removed. Yet again, God had seemed to be speaking to him and guiding him, even before the great moment of conversion.

The importance of this doctrine to Christian spirituality will be obvious. God prepares a way for his coming into our hearts. Just as John the Baptist prepared the way for the coming of the Lord in the wilderness, so God is at work, in the hearts and minds of men and women, preparing them to recognise and receive him. This does not represent an over-riding of human freedom; rather, it amounts to a gentle breaking down of the barriers which naturally come between us and God. God is at work, perhaps in unknown and mysterious ways, among those who have yet to come to faith. Perhaps this may pass unnoticed at the time. But, as countless Christians – Augustine included – can testify, once people come to faith, it is very often possible to discern the ways in which God guided, prepared and challenged them, even before the moment of faith dawned.

CHRISTIAN ETHICS

Not so long ago, there was a movement within liberal theology which argued that there existed a universal morality which Christianity reflected. It was not necessary to know anything about Christian theology to make ethical judgements. This universal morality, it was argued, was adequate in itself. The Christian, Buddhist, Hindu, Moslem, humanist and atheist were all, it was argued, committed to much the same set of moral principles (with unimportant local variations). In his essay *The Abolition of Man*, C.S. Lewis described these as 'the ultimate platitudes of Practical Reason'. That view is now regarded as so seriously vulnerable as to be virtually defunct. Works such as Jeffrey Stout's *Ethics after Babel* destroyed the credibility of the idea of a 'universal morality'. Christian morality – like every other form of morality – is something special and distinct, and not just a sub-species of some non-existent 'universal morality'. With the passing of the myth of a 'universal morality', Christian writers have begun to write with much greater confidence on the theme of 'Christian morality', in the knowledge that there *is* a distinctively Christian outlook on many matters. And this outlook, it is increasingly being stressed, is based upon Christian doctrine.

To make this point, we may consider two highly-acclaimed recent works on the theme of Christian ethics, Oliver O'Donovan's *Resurrection and Moral Order*, and John Mahoney's *The Making of Moral Theology*. Despite differences between the two authors, one theme emerges as of major importance: ethics rests upon doctrine. To give but one example: for O'Donovan, Christian ethics rests upon a proper understanding of the objective order imposed upon creation by God. To *act* in a Christian manner rests upon *thinking* in a Christian manner.

But how does doctrine affect Christian morality? To illustrate the importance of doctrine, we shall consider the way in which four major Christian doctrines have a direct impact upon the way we act.

1. The doctrine of justification by faith

What is the motivation for ethics? Why should we want to do good works of any sort? The doctrine of justification by faith makes two central points of relevance here. First, it stresses that there is no way that our moral actions can earn our salvation. They have no purchasing power in respect to salvation. Second, works are done as a response to our justification. They are a natural expression of thankfulness to God. The *gift* of our justification lays upon us the *obligation* to live in accordance with our new status. We are *made* children of God through our justification as an act of free grace – and now we must act in accordance with this transformation.

The slogan 'become what you are!' neatly summarises this situation, and encapsulates the essence of Pauline ethics with some brilliance. In justification we are made to be the light of the world (Matt. 5:14–16): therefore we must shine out as lights in a dark world, as a city on a hill (Matt. 5:14; Phil. 2:15). We *are* the light of the world; therefore we must *become* the light of the world. Our justification brings about a new obedience – an obedience which would not be conceivable before our justification, and which ultimately rests upon the grace of God.

There is thus an 'automatic' or 'natural' connection between the justification of the sinner and his or her desire and ability to perform good works. The New Testament analogy of the tree and its fruits expresses the fundamental idea that the radical transformation of individuals (and it is worth remembering that the English word 'radical' comes from the Latin *radix*, meaning 'root') is prior to our ability to produce good works. In the Sermon on the Mount, Jesus points out that a good tree bears good fruit, and a bad tree bad fruit (Matt. 7:16–18). The nature of the fruit is biologically determined by the plant itself. Thus grapes don't grow on thorn-bushes, nor do figs grow on thistles. These are just the biological facts of life. If you want to get figs, you have to establish a fig-tree, and get it to fruit.

Underlying these remarkably simple analogies is profound theological insight. The transformation of humanity is a prerequisite for its reformation. Or, as Martin Luther put it, 'it isn't good works which makes an individual good, but a good individual who does good works.' The New Testament, particularly in the Pauline writings, emphasises that this transformation is to be understood as *God's transformation of us*, rather than our own attempt to transform us: thus Paul speaks of the 'fruit of the Spirit' (Gal. 5:22), drawing attention to the fact that this 'fruit' is the result of God's action within us, rather than of our action independent of God. Whereas secular ethical systems tend to discuss moral acts in terms of their goal (in other words, what they achieve, or are intended to achieve), a theological ethical system based upon the doctrine of justification by faith will therefore discuss moral acts in terms of what they *presuppose* or *are intended to express* (in other words, the individual's radical transformation through his conversion). The starting point of an authentically *Christian* ethics is the recognition that the conversion of the individual leads to a new obedience, a new lifestyle and a new ethic.

2. The doctrine of original sin

A central insight of an authentically Christian morality is its realism concerning the limitations of human nature. Where some secular moral thinking degenerates into little more than a blind utopianism, Christian morality addresses the human situation with an informed realism about its strictly limited possibilities. In arguing against an unrealistic reliance upon human reason in ethics, the distinguished Roman Catholic moral theologian Charles Curran remarked that 'the disrupting influence of sin colours all human reality', including human reason itself. Reinhold Niebuhr, perhaps one of the greatest Christian ethical thinkers of the twentieth century, poured scorn on the 'perfectionist illusions' which so confused and misled many liberal Christian thinkers in the 1930s. The doctrine of original sin destroys naive views of human perfectability. There is, according to this doctrine, something inherently *wrong* with human nature, which makes it self-centred, rebellious and disobedient. There is simply no point in informing sinful humanity that the world would be a better place if everyone stopped doing things that are wrong. What is required is a transformation of the human situation so that the motivation for doing wrong is eliminated or reduced. Underlying both the view that the human predicament arises from ignorance and the view that Jesus Christ is nothing more than a good teacher is a remarkably shallow understanding of the nature of humanity itself. As Niebuhr emphasised, all too many modern thinkers tend to work with a remarkably naive view of human nature – probably reflecting the fact that their middle-class intellectual backgrounds tend to inhibit them from encountering and experiencing the darker side of human nature.

The radical realism of the Christian view of sin, and its devastating consequences for our understanding of human beings as moral agents, is captured in the words of Robert Browning, in *Gold Hair:*

> 'Tis the faith that launched point-blank its dart
> At the head of a lie; taught Original Sin,
> The corruption of man's heart.

The bland assumption of the natural goodness of human nature, so characteristic of much western liberal thought, is called into question by this doctrine. The myth of human perfectability and inevitable progress has been shown up for what it is by the savagery and cruelty of the twentieth century. If ever there was a period in human history when human evil was evident, it was the twentieth century. How many outrages such as Auschwitz must we experience before the naïve assumption that all human beings act out of the best of intentions is exposed for what it is – a cruel and seductive lie? Even those who are reluctant to call this inborn and inbuilt discord 'sin' are prepared to recognise its reality – witness the famous words of the atheist poet A. E. Housman:

> The troubles of our proud and angry dust
> Are from eternity, and shall not fail.

The doctrine of original sin brings a breath of refreshing realism to Christian ethics. It allows us to understand that human beings are fallen, with an alarming degree of ability to do evil, knowing that it is evil. The implications of human self-centredness for political institutions (for example, evident in the way in which they can be manipulated and exploited) and moral action will be obvious. Niebuhr's argument for democracy – an excellent example of the political application of a Christian doctrine – was quite simple: it was just about the only way of controlling human self-centredness, and forcing national leaders to respect the needs of others. Put very simply, the doctrine of original sin tells us that morality concerns weak, self-centred and exploitative human beings – in other words, *real* humans, not the perfectable angels of wishful liberal thinking. Power, capital and force – all can be, and will be, abused and exploited for personal ends, unless the political and moral will exists to control them.

Charles Curran also pointed out some central ethical consequences of the Christian doctrine of original sin. Even human reason, the central resource upon which so much secular ethical theory rests, must be regarded as compromised by sin. 'In the total Christian horizon the disrupting influence of sin colours all human reality . . . sin affects reason itself.' Furthermore, sin is so deeply embedded in human nature and society that there are points at which it is impossible to adopt a course of action which avoids sin. The Christian is obliged to choose between two decisions, each of which is sinful. 'In some circumstances the Christian is forced to do something sinful. The sinner reluctantly performs the deed and asks God for forgiveness and mercy.' As Helmut Thielicke argued in his *Theological Ethics*, human society is so thoroughly saturated with sin that Christian ethical decision-making must learn to come to terms with compromise, adjusting to the sinful realities of the world, rather than pretending that an ideal situation exists in which it is possible to draw a clear-cut decision between 'right' and 'wrong'. To pretend that it is possible to make ethical decisions without coming to terms with the severe limitations placed upon human reason and will by sin is to live in a Walter Mitty world of unreality and dreams.

Curran and Thielicke are excellent examples of Christian writers on ethics who are concerned to develop genuinely

Christian approaches to ethical questions, rather than just rehashing secular ideas and values. Time and time again, these writers show the importance of doctrine to ethics. Christian ethics is simply too important to be left to those whose values are determined by the world, rather than by the gospel.

3. The doctrine of creation

Recognition that the world was created by, and now belongs to, God has important consequences for understanding our own responsibilities within that world. We have been placed within God's creation to tend it and take care of it (Gen. 2:15). We may be superior to the remainder of that creation, and exercise authority over it (Ps. 8:4–8) – but we remain under the authority of God, and responsible to him for the way in which we treat his creation. We are the stewards, not the owners, of creation. We hold it in trust. There is a growing realisation today that past generations have seriously abused that trust, exploiting the creation and its resources. There is a real danger that the 'goodness' of creation, including its delicate ecological balances, will be shattered through human greed.

Fortunately, there has been a growing awareness recently of this need to take a more responsible attitude towards creation. Reflecting on our responsibilities as stewards of God's creation is the first step in undoing the harm done by past generations. It matters to God that vast areas of our world are made uninhabitable through nuclear or toxic chemical waste. It matters that the delicate balance of natural forces is disturbed by human carelessness. Sin affects the way we treat the environment as much as it does our attitude towards God, other people, and society as a whole. This Christian doctrine is the basis of a new – and overdue – attitude towards the creation, and our place within it.

4. The doctrine of the incarnation

Some Christians dismiss the suggestion that Christianity involves political or social action. Surely, they say, Christians ought to be concerned about the hereafter rather than the here and now. What reasons may be given for suggesting that Christian ethics, with its vigorous concern for human beings and the creation, is of any importance? Some pointers have already been given in the material already presented; nevertheless, more can be said. Perhaps the doctrine of the incarnation is of supreme importance in this respect.

The doctrine of the incarnation speaks to us of God becoming man. God redeemed his creation from within that creation. He delivered his creatures as one of them. God lodged himself firmly within his creation, in order to redeem it. That same pattern of involvement should be evident in the lives of those redeemed through the coming of Jesus Christ. 'Be imitators of God' (Eph. 5:1).

This phrase serves to emphasise the importance of the incarnation. If we are to be 'imitators of God' (and what a challenging phrase that is!), we need to know what God is like. The doctrine of the incarnation affirms that Jesus Christ tells us in his words, and shows us in his actions, what God is like. For example, Christians are urged to 'love one another' (1 John 4:7–11). This is clearly of some importance for Christian morality. But what does this word 'love' mean? Unless we can spell out what it means and implies, we are left in some doubt about what is required of us.

The doctrine of the incarnation allows us to say what the 'love of God', which we are meant to imitate, looks like. In the image of Jesus Christ, trudging to his lonely place of execution, we are given a model of the love of God. His act of total self-giving, even to the point of death, is the model for true Christian love. He thought not of himself, but of others.

We could take this idea further. Throughout his ministry, we notice Jesus Christ accepting individuals, being prepared to associate with those who were regarded as socially acceptable as much as those who were regarded as social outcasts. The good news of the kingdom was for all, without distinction. That same pattern of divine acceptance should be ours as well. To recognise that Jesus Christ is God incarnate is to recognise that he maps out patterns of behaviour that ought to be characteristic of Christians. Yet we are not saved by imitating Christ; it is by being saved that we are moved to be conformed to his likeness, as we seek to be imitators of God through him.

This brief survey has attempted to show the major impact which doctrine can and must have upon Christian living. The Christian who prays, thinks and worships cannot avoid engaging with matters of doctrine – and the Christian who is doctrinally informed will bring new insights and depth to all these activities. A lack of doctrinal awareness leads to a shallow spirituality and potentially misguided ethics. This point naturally brings us to consider the question of whether it is possible to have 'Christianity without doctrine' in the first place.

8   IS CHRISTIANITY POSSIBLE WITHOUT DOCTRINE?

Many find themselves attracted to the idea of 'Christianity without dogma'. Christianity, they might argue, is a practical religion. The Sermon on the Mount, they might suggest, lies at the centre of the Christian faith, rather than Paul's theology or its development in the Christian tradition. The gospel is moral, or it is nothing. Christianity is about bringing into the modern world the same breadth of spirit, the same compassion and care, the same depth of spiritual awareness, that was first shown to the world in the person of Jesus of Nazareth. Christianity is about action and attitudes, not about the cold, barren and outdated world of dogmas. Especially in the late nineteenth century, there were many writers who argued that Christianity was basically nothing more and nothing less than the personal religion of Jesus. We were called to share his faith in God. We should not believe *in* Jesus, but *with* Jesus.

There will be many who will feel sympathy with such views. Indeed, if I may be allowed to share a personal memory, I once held them strongly myself. I no longer do so, and believe that I was seriously (but sincerely) mistaken in accepting this radical devaluation of doctrine. Like many a young man, I found the romantic image of a 'Christianity without doctrine' profoundly attractive. It seemed to represent the best of all possible worlds, combining a rhetorical appeal to the great western liberal deities of intellectual freedom and personal integrity with an unashamed, almost mystical, sentimental fascination, focused upon the distant hero-figure of Jesus himself. Here was a living person, whose gospel consisted in the simplicities of commitment and obedience. The demand to follow him was a call to imitate him in his relation to God and to others. We are called to imitate him, to copy him, to pattern ourselves upon him.

Simple solutions are attractive, yet seductive. As I reflected upon my early understanding of Christianity, I began to appreciate how intellectually shallow it was. 'Christianity without doctrine' seemed to me increasingly untenable. In the remainder of this chapter, I shall outline some of the difficulties which persuaded me to abandon my belief in this idea. Inevitably, ideas and arguments which have been deployed earlier in this work may re-appear, in slightly different forms, in this chapter; it is, however, important that they should be marshalled together in dealing with this important question. Some of these arguments are mutually related, others are not. They seem to me, however, to build up to give a decisive cumulative case against the possibility of a 'Christianity without doctrine'.

1. Believing in Jesus – not with Jesus

It is impossible to speak about Christians copying the private relationship of Jesus to his Father (a classic belief of the 'Christianity without doctrine' school) without noting that Jesus spells out, in sermon and parable, what that relationship presupposes, expresses and demands.

If Christianity is simply about Christians imitating Jesus' relation to God, we are confronted with two major obstacles. First, we are told remarkably little about it in the New Testament itself. What form did it take? The Gospels are silent, apparently reflecting a silence on the part of Jesus himself. Jesus withdrew from the crowd to be with his Father in prayer, and if we were ever meant to know the full details of his personal relationship with the Father (which is highly unlikely), that knowledge has been denied to us. In the second place, what we do know about Jesus' relationship with his Father puts it beyond us. It is not transferable to believers. We cannot share in its fullness. Jesus' relationship with the Father reflects who Jesus is – and we can never share his unique identity and thus his relationship.

In any case, the history of Christianity shows no evidence of Christians ever believing that they were called to mimic the faith of Jesus. Rather, we find faith in and worship of a risen, redeeming and glorified Christ. Christ is someone in whom we can trust, but one whom we can only imitate very poorly – and in his relationship to God, we cannot imitate him at all. If we are the children of God, it is not in the same sense as Jesus was the Son of God. The gospel is not about copying Jesus, or repeating his experiences – it is, as it always has been, about appropriating Jesus. We come to God in Christ and through Christ – not with Jesus.

This view of Christ as a religious example is closely linked with a deficient view of human nature, which does not – or *will* not – come to terms with the sheer intractability of the fact of human sin, and the strange and tragic history of humanity in general, and the Christian church in particular. As Bishop Charles Gore pointed out incisively a century ago:

> Inadequate conceptions of Christ's person go hand in hand with inadequate conceptions of what human nature wants. The Nestorian conception of Christ . . . qualifies Christ for being an example of what man can do, and into what wonderful union with God he can be assumed if he is holy enough; but Christ remains one man among many, shut in within the limits of a single human personality, and influencing man only from outside. He can be a Redeemer of man if man can be saved from outside by bright example, but not otherwise. The Nestorian Christ is logically associated with the Pelagian man . . . The

Nestorian Christ is the fitting Saviour of the Pelagian man.

In other words, a Nestorian Christology (that is, a view of Jesus Christ which regards him primarily as a human example worthy of imitation) is linked with a Pelagian doctrine of human nature (that is, the idea that human beings are perfectly capable of attaining salvation without divine aid, except in the general area of being provided with guidance and examples of what is required of them).

Jesus must be more than just a religious teacher to account for his position within Christianity. C.S. Lewis expressed this point clearly and trenchantly:

> We have never followed the advice of great teachers. Why are we likely to begin now? Why are we more likely to follow Christ than any of the others? Because he's the best moral teacher? But that makes it even less likely that we shall follow him. If Christianity only means one more bit of good advice, then Christianity is of no importance. There's been no lack of good advice over the last four thousand years. A bit more makes no difference.

In fact, however, Christians do not speak of Jesus in this way, as Lewis stresses. They speak of being 'saved' through him. They speak about encountering God through him.

In any case, the teaching of Jesus himself carries us beyond the idea that Jesus is only a teacher. The outrage provoked by Jesus among his Jewish audience when he declared that the paralytic's sins were forgiven (Mark 2:5) was utterly genuine. Their theology was utterly correct: 'Who can forgive sins but God alone?' (Mark 2:7). Jesus' words point back to himself. If they are to be taken seriously, they amount to a remarkable statement concerning Jesus himself. His identity and status become part of this message. His statements about God are mingled with statements concerning himself, even to the point where the reliability and trustworthiness of the former come to depend upon the latter. The statements concerning what Jesus believes himself to be called and able to do require clarification of the relationship between Jesus and God, between the Son and the Father – and thus point to the need for doctrines, such as that of the incarnation.

2. The authority of Jesus rests upon doctrinal beliefs concerning him

To allow that Jesus is a religious teacher is to raise the question of his authority. Why should we take him seriously? We have been fortunate enough to have had the advice of countless moral and religious teachers in human history – what makes Jesus different? What singles him out as commanding attention? As we have already seen (pp. 4–6), it is untenable to suggest that Jesus' authority rests upon the excellence of his moral or religious teaching. To make this suggestion is to imply that Jesus has authority only when he happens to agree with us. We thus would have authority over Jesus.

In fact, however, the teaching of Jesus has authority on account of who Jesus is – and the identity and significance of Jesus can only be spelled out in doctrinal terms. 'We cannot go on treating and believing in Jesus Christ in a way in which it would be wrong to treat and believe in another man, without a theory of his person that explains that he is something more than man' (Charles Gore). It is doctrine which explains why and how Jesus' words and deeds have divine, rather than purely human, authority. It is doctrine which singles out Jesus Christ, and none other, as being God incarnate. To pay attention to Jesus Christ reflects our fundamental conviction that God speaks through this man as through no other. Here is no prophet, speaking on God's behalf at second-hand; here is God himself, speaking to us. 'We have to do with God himself as we have to do with this man. God himself speaks when this man speaks in human speech' (Karl Barth). Quite contrary to the Broad

Church liberals of the nineteenth century (who believed it was possible to uphold the religious and ethical aspects of Christianity, while discarding its doctrines), the authority of Jesus' moral and religious teaching thus rests firmly upon a doctrinal foundation.

This point is made with care and persuasion by the distinguished Oxford philosopher of religion Basil Mitchell. In his essay 'Is there a distinctive Christian ethic?', Mitchell stresses that ethics depend upon world-views – and that world-views in turn depend upon doctrine.

> Any world-view which carries with it important implications for our understanding of man and his place in the universe would yield its own distinctive insights into the scope, character and content of morality. To answer the further question, 'What *is* the distinctive Christian ethic?', is inevitably to be involved to some extent in controversial questions of Christian doctrine.

The 'Christianity without doctrine' school thus finds itself in something of a quandary. If Christianity is primarily about certain religious or moral attitudes, it seems that those attitudes rest upon doctrinal presuppositions. Doctrine determines attitudes. It is utterly pointless to argue that we all ought to imitate the religious and moral attitudes of Jesus – that is a demand for blind and unthinking obedience. The question of *why* we should regard these attitudes as being authoritative demands to be considered. And that means explaining what it is about Jesus Christ as singling him out as authoritative – in short, developing doctrines about Jesus.

This point was made clearly and prophetically by William Temple. Writing against the 'Religion without Dogma' movement in 1942, he declared that:

> You would hardly find any theologian now who supposes that Christian ethics can survive for half a century in

detachment from Christian doctrine, and this is the very last moment when the church itself can come forward with outlines of Christian ethics in the absence of the theological foundation which alone makes them really tenable. Our people have grown up in a generally Christian atmosphere, and take it for granted that all people who are not actually perverted hold what are essentially Christian notions about human conduct. But this is not true.

(Temple then goes on to illustrate this point with reference to the rise of Hitler and Stalin in the 1930s.) Although many liberal and radical writers of the 1960s suggested that Christian ethics could be divorced from doctrine, and maintain an independent existence, the wisdom of Temple's words is once more apparent. Distinctive *ethics* (whether Marxist, Christian or Buddhist) are dependent upon *world-views*, which are in turn shaped by *doctrines*, by understandings of human nature and destiny.

What we might call the 'common-sense-Christianity' school will probably continue to insist that faith is a 'practical and down-to-earth matter', having nothing to do with 'airy-fairy theories' (if I might use phrases I was fond of myself at one time). The famous economist J. M. Keynes came across similar attitudes among industrialists and politicians. 'We're practical people', they declared, 'who have no need for abstract theories about economics'. Yet these people, Keynes scathingly remarked, were little more than the unwitting slaves of some defunct economist. Their allegedly 'practical' outlook actually rested upon unacknowledged economic theories. They lacked the insight to see that what they regarded as obvious was actually based upon the theories of some long-dead economist. Without knowing it, 'common-sense-Christianity' rests upon quite definite doctrinal foundations. The man who declares, in the name of common sense, that 'Jesus was simply a good man', may genuinely believe that he has avoided matters of doctrine – whereas he has actually echoed the doctrines of the

Enlightenment. The study of Christian doctrine is thus profoundly liberating, as it exposes these hidden doctrinal assumptions. Every version of Christianity that has ever existed rests upon doctrinal foundations; not every version of Christianity has grasped this fact. The genuine question of importance is quite simple: which of those doctrinal foundations is the most authentic and reliable?

3. The gospel itself rests upon a doctrinal framework

Why is Christianity good news? In part, because it proclaims the reality of the love of God to the world. It points to Jesus Christ upon the cross, and declares, 'God loved the world this much' (see John 3:16). But the death of Jesus Christ upon the cross is only good news if it is interpreted in a certain way.

Doctrine defines how the cross of Christ is to be interpreted. To put it another way, it provides an interpretative framework for understanding the events of Calvary. It is not good news if a man, after a life of self-giving and care for his fellows, should be harried, tortured, mocked and finally executed in a triumphant display of barbarity. It is no gospel if this man reveals the love of one human being for another, far far away and long long ago. It only becomes good news if it is interpreted in a certain way. It becomes good news if it is the Son of God himself who gives himself in order that we might come to newness of life. It becomes good news if these events are interpreted in terms of a sufficiently high profile of identity between Jesus and God, such as that set out by the doctrine of the incarnation.

Doctrine aims to explain what it is about the life, death and resurrection of Jesus Christ which is good news. It aims to explain and justify the vital connection between the 'there and then' of Calvary and the 'here and now' of our own situation. It is an interpretative bridge between history and faith, between the past and the present. It relates the events of Calvary to our own experience, interpreting the latter in terms of the former.

4. Doctrine defines what manner of response is appropriate to the gospel

What must we do to be saved? What sort of response is appropriate to the gospel? What conditions must be met before the renewal promised in Jesus Christ can be actualised in our lives? To answer these questions – even if the answer proposed is 'nothing' – is to make vitally important doctrinal statements. Enormous decisions, affecting our manner of life, depend upon these doctrinal presuppositions.

To illustrate this point, we shall consider the events surrounding a small group of Italian noblemen in the early sixteenth century. The group, all of whom were educated at the University of Padua, met regularly, to discuss the question of how they might be saved. They were confused – hardly surprisingly, as the church had gone through a long period of confusion in relation to the doctrine of justification. No-one could say, with any great degree of certainty, what an individual had to do in order to be saved. This alarming degree of uncertainty was reflected in Martin Luther's anxieties about his own spiritual situation, which would eventually boil over into the Lutheran Reformation.

In the year 1510, the small group of Italian noblemen split into two. They had been unable to reach agreement on what their response to the gospel ought to be. One section of the group (the larger), centering on Paolo Giustiniani, entered a local monastery, there to work out their salvation under conditions of the utmost austerity. Only in this way, they believed, could they be sure of gaining salvation. The smaller section, centering on Gasparo Contarini, believed that they could gain salvation while remaining in the everyday world. It was only later that the confusion was resolved, in the aftermath of the Reformation: it was possible to be saved through responding to the gospel in faith, while remaining active in the world.

The doctrine of justification by faith spells out what response is required of individuals, if they are to benefit from the death and resurrection of Jesus Christ. This doctrinal framework is essential: we must know what is demanded of us, if we are to be reconciled to God and receive newness of life. As the Reformation made abundantly clear, to be vague in this respect is disastrous, both spiritually and theologically. It is of no value to be able to give a full account of all the benefits and challenges the gospel brings, without being able to explain how that gospel may be received. Doubts about whether one has made the appropriate response to the gospel will inevitably lead to spiritual paralysis through doubt and confusion.

A similar point was made by the philosopher Immanuel Kant, in his work *Religion within the Limits of Reason Alone*. Kant stressed that, unless an individual could know that past sins had been forgiven and moral guilt cancelled, it was virtually impossible for him or her to live a moral life. It was only when this individual knew that the guilt of the past had been cancelled that moral improvement could begin. Doubts about whether forgiveness had *really* been granted could thus completely wreck an individual's life. They would bring about a form of moral paralysis. For such reasons, Kant insisted that individuals should be able to *be assured* of the forgiveness of their past sins, in order that they might get on with the business of leading new lives.

Precisely the same point must be made in connection with faith. The believer must know that he or she has been forgiven, and accepted by God. It is only when we are sure that we really have begun the Christian life that we can begin to pay full attention to what the Christian life demands. Our personal living out of the gospel depends on being able to rest secure that we stand within the gospel. A doctrine which makes clear what we must *do* in order to begin the Christian life is thus an essential and proper precondition for all Christian morality and spirituality.

5. Doctrine is the proper outcome of reflection on faith

Human beings are rational creatures. They ask questions – questions like 'Why?' As Plato stressed, there is a natural human desire to 'give an account of things'. Why are we being asked to accept the teachings of Jesus Christ? Why is he singled out among other human beings? Psychologists have pointed out that there seems to be some basic human need to *attribute* meaning to events. 'Attributional processes' seem to be a normal part of human reflection upon the puzzles of human existence, in an attempt to make sense of it all. This need to make sense of things applies equally to matters of Christian faith. For example, the crucifixion and resurrection are things which need to be explained. Why did they happen? What do they mean?

In his 1891 Bampton Lectures, delivered at Oxford University, Charles Gore pointed out that this natural human inquisitiveness has its religious outcome in doctrine.

> Christians found themselves treating Jesus Christ, believing in Jesus Christ, as they had never treated or believed in any other man . . . Because they were rational they must have asked themselves 'Why do we treat Jesus Christ in this exceptional manner? Who is he to be so treated? What is his relation to God whose functions he exercises? Why are we not idolaters if we yield him such worship?' They must have asked these questions because they were men endowed with reason, and could not therefore go on acting without giving some account of their action.

Doctrine is nothing other than the attempt of rational believers to make sense of every aspect of their experience of Jesus Christ. If conversion involves the mind as well as the soul, doctrine is its inevitable outcome, as the believer brings his or her mind to bear on the implications of faith.

The eleventh-century writer Anselm of Canterbury had a neat way of expressing this. He spoke of 'faith seeking understanding'. Once you come to faith, you aim to understand what you have believed. Faith comes first, and is followed by understanding. Doctrine results from this attempt to understand what has been believed. It attempts to make explicit the implicit assumptions of faith. For example, faith believes that we have been saved through Jesus Christ; doctrine asserts that this belief implies that Jesus must be both God and man if this is to be possible. Doctrine is basically the outcome of taking rational trouble over the mysteries of faith. To prohibit this rational reflection in order to develop a 'Christianity without doctrine' is to deny Christians the right to think about their faith. Doctrinal reflection is the product of a passionate search for truth, combining intellectual curiosity and honesty.

This chapter has outlined in the briefest of manners some of the reasons for thinking that doctrine is a proper and necessary element of Christianity. The idea of a 'Christianity without doctrine' may, on first inspection, seem both plausible and attractive. On closer examination, however, this proves to be a profoundly misleading impression. Even the very brief points made in the present chapter must go some way towards suggesting that doctrine serves a vital purpose.

This is not to say that Christianity is only about doctrine. As we have stressed throughout this book, an experience of God through Jesus Christ lies at the heart of the Christian faith. Doctrine is only one aspect of that faith. It is, however, a vital aspect. It is like the bones which give strength and shape to the human body. It is like the steel rods which reinforce concrete structures. Without doctrine, faith becomes shapeless, weak and vulnerable. Doctrine addresses, interprets and transforms human experience, in order that a dynamic, living and resilient faith may result.

In a later chapter, we will look at one of the more helpful

ways of getting to grips with doctrine in this way. It is by studying the creeds that a new appreciation of the depths and richness of the Christian faith can come about. However, another question demands to be considered more pressingly. Any volume which deals with the subject of doctrine ought to deal with one of the great taboo areas of modern Christian theology – heresy. What *is* heresy, and why is so much importance attached to it? It is this difficult and sensitive subject, hardly even touched upon in modern theological writings, which we shall consider in the next chapter.

9 THE COHERENCE OF DOCTRINE AND THE CHALLENGE OF HERESY

The very word 'heresy' is unfashionable. It rarely enters the vocabulary of many modern Christian writers. Even to suggest that an individual's views are 'heretical' is to risk being scorned for holding on to thoroughly outdated ideas. Even to mention the word 'heresy' is to court the charge of being 'medieval' or 'authoritarian'. It must be said that these charges have much to commend them. Many of the more recent heresy trials have been little less than disgraceful, often showing up the prosecutors as dogmatic and small-minded individuals, with little real understanding of the Christian gospel.

An example might be given to make this point. One of the greatest works of Scottish theology in the nineteenth century was John McLeod Campbell's *Nature of the Atonement*, published in 1856. Yet this same individual had been tried for heresy by the Church of Scotland a quarter of a century earlier. While minister at the village of Rhu on the Gare Loch, Campbell had preached that God's saving grace is offered to all, and not just to the elect. Some members of his congregation took notes of these sermons. Among Campbell's statements thus recorded was 'The person who knows that Christ died for every human being is the person who is in a condition to go forth to every human being and say, "Let there be peace between you and God!"' This clearly taught that Christ died for all sinners, and not just for the predestined few – and thus contradicted the Westminster Confession of faith, a sixteenth-century document whose statements were at that time rigorously upheld within the Scottish kirk.

The note-takers complained with 'detestation and abhorrence' that their minister was preaching heresy. The case finally came to the General Assembly of the Church of Scotland in 1831. After an all-night sitting, the Assembly declared, by a majority of 119 to six, that he had taught 'doctrines at variance with the Word of God and the standards of the Church of Scotland'. It imposed the most severe penalty at its disposal. He was to cease to be a minister of the Church. Needless to say, the Church of Scotland would later relax its strict views on this particular doctrine (often known as 'limited atonement'), which is not explicitly stated in Scripture. By then, however, Campbell was dead. This welcome development was too late to be of any interest to him.

Countless other such cases could be instanced. The notion of heresy, and all the apparatus of heresy trials to which it gave rise, seem to be firmly erased from much modern Christian thinking. I wish to suggest, however, that the idea of heresy remains important for the Christian churches. Neither the word nor the ideas should be allowed to be abolished or forgotten, as if they were of purely antiquarian interest. This is not for one moment to suggest that legal action, criminal or civil, should be taken against individuals who might be regarded as heretical. Rather, it is to affirm that the theological notion of heresy can still be of considerable service in maintaining the faithfulness of the Christian church to her calling.

Let us begin by considering what the term originally meant. The Greek word *haeresis*, as used within the New Testament, can have the more or less neutral sense of 'party' or 'faction' (Acts 5:17; 15:5; 26:5). However, the word can also have a developed meaning – a party or faction which arises through a defective understanding of the Christian faith (1 Cor. 11:19; Gal. 5:20). It is not simply doctrinal disagreement which made a heresy; it is the threat which it posed to the unity of the Christian church. By the fourth century, however, the word had acquired a developed meaning, more or less equivalent to the present-day meaning of the word. 'Orthodoxy' (that is, 'holding right views') became established as the opposite of heresy.

What does the word heresy designate? To begin with, let us draw a distinction between *unbelief* and *heresy*. Unbelief, it must be stressed, is not a heresy. Walter Kaufmann entitled his personal atheistic manifesto *The Faith of a Heretic*. In fact, the title is quite inappropriate. Atheism is no heresy; it is simply a non-Christian belief. To understand the importance of heresy, and the particular challenge and difficulties it poses for Christianity, it is necessary to realise that heresy is a form of belief. Orthodoxy and heresy are both sub-categories of Christian faith. Heresy is something which arises within the context of faith. We could represent the situation diagramatically as in Figure 2.

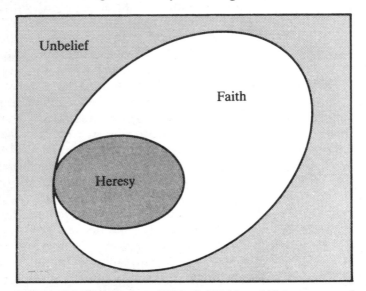

FIGURE 2 The Relation of Unbelief, Faith and Heresy

It is thus quite incorrect to suggest that atheism, agnosticism, Islam or Hinduism are in any way heresies. (It is certainly true that the Spanish Inquisition regarded Moslems and Protestants alike as heretics – but this reflects the politicised idea of heresy associated with the Middle Ages. We are here concerned with reclaiming the authentically theological sense of the term, which involves setting to one side such distortions of the notion as are associated with the Inquisition.)

As the diagram indicates, unbelief could be defined as the rejection of the central cluster of Christian beliefs centering on the redemptive action of God through Jesus Christ. To deny that God redeems us through Jesus Christ is not strictly heresy; it is more a form of unbelief. Heresy arises through accepting the basic cluster of Christian beliefs – yet interpreting them in such a way that inconsistency results. A heresy is thus an inadequate or deficient form of Christianity. By its very deficiency, it poses a threat to the gospel.

This difficult point needs illustration. Let us consider the statement: human beings are reconciled to God only through Jesus Christ. This is a central insight of the New Testament. To deny it is to place oneself outside the boundaries of the Christian church. It is to identify oneself as a non-Christian. This is not to make any moral judgement about the person wishing to do this, nor to make any statement concerning the intellectual merits of the case. It is simply to say that the holding of certain views inevitably means declaring that one does not share central Christian presuppositions and, for that reason, cannot in all integrity be regarded as a Christian. The word 'Christian' cannot be allowed to become so vague that it allows anyone, irrespective of his or her views, to be considered a Christian. As we stressed in an earlier chapter (pp. 57–65), doctrine functions as a social demarcator, laying down criteria for determining who is a member of the Christian community, and who is not.

To accept and act upon this belief, that human beings are reconciled to God only through Jesus Christ, is to declare that one stands within the community of faith. But there now arises the question of how this statement is to be interpreted. Heresy arises through inadequate understandings of central Christian beliefs. An example, arising from the belief just mentioned and centering upon the identity of Jesus Christ, may prove helpful.

Suppose you held that Jesus Christ is just a good man, like any other human being. He might be a particularly fine teacher, or a morally outstanding individual. Nevertheless, he is *only* a man, differing from us in degree, rather than kind. What is the result of this belief? The answer is that it makes the belief, that human beings are reconciled to God only through Jesus Christ, internally inconsistent. There is a fatal contradiction within it. For if Jesus is just a human being like us, he shares our common condition. He is not so much the solution to our problem, as part of it. Either he cannot do anything about the situation, or else he can only change it to the extent that any other human being can. But the emphasis upon the fact that our situation *has* been changed, and *only* changed through Jesus Christ, is inconsistent with this belief concerning the identity of Jesus. If Jesus Christ is only human, we cannot be reconciled to God through him. And so doubt is cast over a central premise of the Christian faith. Why? Because it is shown to be inconsistent with another belief. Either one or the other is wrong. They cannot both be right. To maintain that both are correct is impossible. There is a serious deficiency somewhere along the line.

Heresy arises through inconsistency. It arises through beliefs which are in conflict with the central Christian affirmation of redemption in Jesus Christ. All the major heresies of the Christian faith centre upon precisely this principle. Let us consider two classic fourth-century heresies to make this point clearer.

ARIANISM

This heresy declared that Jesus Christ was a creature, not God incarnate. In many ways, Arius was forced to this conclusion by his acceptance of the classical Greek view of God as unchangeable, which he found to be irreconcilable with the Christian doctrine of the incarnation. Despite what is often said about him, Arius was a reluctant heretic, forced to make a momentous choice between Christian and classical Greek views of God – and feeling obliged to opt for the latter. Arius affirmed that it was possible to refer to Jesus as 'Son of God', but in a purely honorary manner. To do this was just a way of being polite about Christ. Jesus is pre-eminent among all God's creatures – but is still a created being. He is not, and cannot be thought of, as being God incarnate.

This caused a radical inconsistency within the Christian doctrine of salvation, as Arius' opponent, Athanasius, was quick to point out. It meant that one creature (Jesus Christ) was held to be able to redeem other creatures (sinners). Yet only God could save. Either salvation was thus an impossibility, or there was something radically wrong with Arius' understanding of the identity of Jesus Christ. It was fatally flawed at some point. Yet, as Arius was perfectly prepared to accept that we are redeemed only through Jesus Christ, the fault had to lie with an inadequate understanding of the identity of Jesus Christ. It was only through allowing that Jesus Christ was both God and man that redemption could be safeguarded. Arius' ideas posed a serious threat to the Christian doctrine of salvation.

APOLLINARIANISM

Apollinarius felt that the dignity of Jesus Christ was compromised by the suggestion that he was fully human. If Jesus Christ was totally human, he argued, he would have a normal human mind, subject to all the temptations and unpleasant thoughts that human beings are prone to have. This was unthinkable. So, in a thoroughly well-intentioned effort to preserve the dignity of Christ, Apollinarius argued that Jesus must have had a divine, rather than a human, mind. This was vigorously challenged by his opponent, Gregory of Nazianzen. On the basis of his maxim 'the unassumed is the unhealed', Gregory argued that Christ must have had a human mind. Otherwise, the human mind was unredeemed. Part of our human nature (and a very important part of that) would have been left unaffected by the incarnation. A vital section of our humanity would have been unredeemed. Once more, heresy was seen to be an inadequate statement of the Christian faith.

Heresy is thus clearly seen to be a defective version of Christianity. It is a version of Christianity, in the sense that it accepts the major premises of faith – which distinguishes it from unbelief, or non-Christian beliefs. But precisely because it is inadequate, it poses a threat to Christianity. Thomas Carlyle once wrote that, 'if Arianism had won, Christianity would have dwindled to a legend.' There is much truth in the old Latin proverb, *corruptio optimi pessimum est*, 'there is nothing worse than the corruption of the best.'

Heresy is simply second-rate Christianity. Heresy might be good in comparison with unbelief – but it had to give way to something which was better. As Voltaire remarked, 'the best is the enemy of the good.' And, if Christianity is to survive, let alone to prosper, it must confront a hostile world with all its resources fully available. The early church was so concerned about the threat posed by heresy, on account of its perilous situation. It felt itself to be continually under threat from an aggressive pagan culture. Its future depended upon its intellectual credibility on the one hand, and its internal unity on the other. Heresy destabilised the church, both intellectually and socially.

It is right that every age should reconsider the classic heresies, in order to establish whether they really are fatally flawed. Orthodoxy is not something which demands to be believed on blind trust – it has a theological case to make, by demonstrating its superiority over heretical versions of Christianity. Each generation will wish to convince itself of the rightness of the evaluation of heresies and orthodoxy made by previous generations. But all the indications are that the classical heresies will continue to be considered deficient and inadequate versions of the gospel.

This analysis also draws attention to the importance of internal consistency. Doctrines are not stated or developed in isolation. They interact with one another. Rightly understood, there is a wonderful coherence to Christian doctrine. We could explore this further by returning to the principle which we explored earlier, that human beings are reconciled to God only through Jesus Christ. Let us briefly consider this further.

We have already seen how this principle necessitates certain central beliefs concerning Jesus Christ. He must be fully human and fully divine; otherwise, radical inconsistency arises within the principle. This shows the close connection between the doctrine of salvation and the doctrine of the two natures of Jesus Christ. It also provides a vital stimulus, which eventually leads to the doctrine of the Trinity. If Jesus is God, any simple idea of God is shown to be inadequate. The Christian doctrine of God must be capable of doing justice to the divinity of Christ. Considerations along these lines eventually lead to the classic Christian statement on the nature of God – the doctrine of the Trinity. The principle also necessitates important insights concerning human nature. For example, the assertion that Jesus Christ is the saviour of all human beings naturally implies that all human beings need to be saved. Latent within the doctrine of the universal redemption of humanity through Jesus Christ is the doctrine of the universal sinfulness of humanity – in other words, the basis of a doctrine of original sin.

This analysis could be extended. However, the basic point is clear. Consistency and coherence are vitally important to

Christian doctrine. Doctrines cannot be considered in isolation; they must be considered in relation to other doctrines,
and in relation to the central reality which they claim to
interpret to the best of their ability – Jesus Christ. It is
not as if this consistency has to be invented; it is already
given. It is not as if the coherence of Christian doctrine
is imposed upon that doctrine; it is already inherent within
it. It is the task of responsible doctrinal reflection to ensure
that this coherence is not disrupted or compromised through
inadequate or deficient statements of key doctrines – such
as Arianism. It is probably impossible to get rid of all the
unhelpful associations of the word 'heresy'. But it continues
to be an important and usable concept – if it is rightly
understood.

We may summarise the present discussion in this way.
Heresy is an inauthentic and inadequate account of the
Christian faith, whose inauthenticity and inadequacy are
disclosed by critical comparison with orthodoxy. Orthodoxy
is not, and never must become, something which is enforced
by law or by force. It is something which, like truth itself,
commends itself by its inner coherence and credibility. The
history of the Christian faith suggests that it cannot risk
being weakened by allowing inadequate versions of the
gospel to pass as authentic. There is a need for each and
every generation to reclaim the concept of heresy, in its
legitimate form, having the courage to suggest that certain
presentations of Christianity are just not good enough.

This means that Christians must be encouraged to wrestle
with matters of doctrine, and to see why certain versions of
Christianity are unnecessarily weak. In an earlier chapter, we
mentioned that wrestling with the creeds is perhaps one of
the best ways of coming to grips with doctrine. We shall now
turn to consider how these central Christian declarations of
faith can help in this way.

10 WRESTLING WITH DOCTRINE: DISCOVERING THE CREEDS

The creeds are well known to most Christians, not least through having become incorporated into various set forms of worship. During the twentieth century, the creeds have gained new importance, as they have increasingly become seen as stressing the unity that exists between Christians. In 1920, the Lambeth Conference recognised the Apostles' Creed as one of the four pillars of Christian unity. In 1927, the World Conference of Faith and Order, meeting at Lausanne, declared that this creed could be used wholeheartedly by Christians of all persuasions. Whatever may divide one group of Christians from another, the creeds provide a summary of the points which unite them.

The oldest and simplest creed of the church is generally known as the Apostles' Creed. All Christian churches recognise its authority and its importance as a standard of doctrine. To study the Apostles' Creed is to investigate a central element of our common Christian heritage. It is an affirmation of the basic beliefs which unite Christians throughout the world and across the centuries. Its text runs as follows:

I believe in God, the Father almighty, creator of heaven and earth. I believe in Jesus Christ, his only Son, our Lord. He was conceived by the power of the Holy Spirit, and born of the Virgin Mary. He suffered under Pontius Pilate, was crucified, died and was buried. He descended to the dead. On the third day he rose again. He ascended into heaven, and is seated at the right hand of the Father. He will come again to judge the living and the dead. I believe in the Holy Spirit, the holy catholic church, the communion of saints, the forgiveness of sins, the resurrection of the body, and the life everlasting. Amen.

The Apostles' Creed, however, was not the only creed to come into existence in the period of the early church. Two major controversies in the early church made it necessary to be more precise about certain matters of doctrine. The first controversy (the Arian controversy of the fourth century) centred on the relationship of Jesus and God. In order to avoid inadequate understandings of the relation of the Father and the Son, the Council of Chalcedon (AD 451) endorsed a creed now generally known as the 'Nicene Creed'. This creed, roughly twice as long as the Apostles' Creed, begins with the words 'We believe in one God.' In its efforts to insist upon the reality of the divinity of Jesus Christ, this creed speaks of Jesus as 'being of one substance with the Father'. It includes important amplifications of the Christian doctrine both of the person of Christ and of the person and work of the Holy Spirit.

A second major controversy shortly afterwards centred on the doctrine of the Trinity. In order to avoid inadequate understandings of the relation of the Father, Son and Spirit, the formula generally known as the 'Athanasian Creed' was drawn up. This creed, which opens with the words 'Whoever wishes to be saved . . .', is by far the longest of the three creeds, and is nowadays rarely used in any form of public worship.

THE ORIGINS OF THE CREEDS

The origins of the creeds may be found within the New Testament itself. There are frequent calls to be 'baptised in the name of Jesus Christ' (Acts 2:38; 8:12; 10:48), or 'in the name of the Lord Jesus' (Acts 8:16; 19:5). In its simplest form, the earliest Christian creed seems to have been simply the declaration that 'Jesus is Lord!' (Rom. 10:9; 1 Cor. 12:3; 2 Cor. 4:5; Phil. 2:11). Anyone who was able to make this declaration was regarded as being a Christian. The Christian is thus someone who 'receives Jesus Christ as Lord' (Col. 2:6).

To declare that 'Jesus Christ is Lord' involves two related claims. In the first place, it declares the believer's loyalty and commitment to Jesus Christ. For someone to confess that 'Jesus Christ is Lord' is to declare that Jesus is the Lord of his or her life. To recognise that Jesus is Lord is to seek to do his will. The refusal of the first Christians to worship the Roman emperor reflects this belief: you can serve only one master, and for the Christian that is, and can only be, none other than Jesus himself. Much the same situation arose in Nazi Germany, eventually giving rise to the Barmen Declaration (p. 12), perhaps one of the most powerful modern statements of the Lordship of Christ over his church.

In the second place, 'Jesus is Lord' declares certain things about Jesus, especially his relation to God. 'Let all Israel be assured of this: God has made this Jesus, whom you cruci-fied, both Lord and Christ' (Acts 2:36). With these words, Peter echoes the common teaching of the New Testament – through the resurrection of Jesus, God has established his credentials as both Messiah and the Lord. The Old Testament frequently uses the term 'Lord' to refer to God (e.g., Gen. 12:1; 15:6; 17:1; 39:2; Exod. 3:2). When the Old Testament scriptures were translated from Hebrew into Greek, the Greek word *kyrios* – 'the Lord' – was used to translate the sacred name of God. But an astonishing new development takes place in the New Testament: it is now *Jesus* who is regularly referred to as 'the Lord' (e.g., Phil. 2:11; 3:8; Col. 2:6). A word which was once used to refer to God has now come to refer to Jesus.

As time went on, however, it became necessary to explain

what Christians believed about Jesus Christ in more detail. The full implications of declaring that 'Jesus is Lord' needed to be spelled out. What did Christians believe about God? about Jesus? about the Holy Spirit? By the fourth century, the Apostles' Creed as we now know it had assumed a more or less fixed form; what variations did exist were slight, and were finally eliminated in the seventh century. Although it was not actually written by the apostles, the Apostles' Creed is a splendid summary of the apostolic teaching concerning the gospel. It lists a series of central doctrines, which may be regarded as fundamental to the Christian faith. The Nicene Creed includes important additional material relating to Christ and the Holy Spirit, allowing certain misunderstandings to be avoided. The creeds are the classical expression of what Christians believe about God and Jesus Christ. In short, they provide a shorthand account of the central doctrines of the Christian faith.

In an earlier chapter, we pointed out that a distinction could be made between 'fundamental' or 'essential' doctrines, and those which were of lesser importance. Many writers have suggested that the doctrines of the creed are the fundamental doctrines of the Christian faith – the doctrines which bind Christians together down the ages and across the world, and which must be defended in the face of an external or internal threat. Others, however, have suggested that other doctrines need to be added to provide a more complete picture of the Christian faith – for example, a doctrine of original sin, or a more explicit doctrine of redemption, or a more detailed account of the identity and status of the sources of Christian doctrine (such as Scripture).

THE PURPOSE OF THE CREEDS

The Apostles' Creed had its origins in the early church as a profession or confession of faith made by converts at their baptism. The early church placed great emphasis upon the importance of the baptism of converts. During the period of Lent (the period from Ash Wednesday to Easter), those who had recently come to faith were given instruction in the Christian faith. Finally, when they had mastered the basics of faith, they would recite the Apostles' Creed together, as a corporate witness to the faith in which they believed, and which they now understood. Faith had now been reinforced with understanding. These converts would then be baptised with great ceremony and joy on Easter Day itself, as the church celebrated the resurrection of its Lord and Saviour. In this way, the significance of the baptism of the believer could be fully appreciated: he or she had passed from death to life (Rom. 6:3–10). Baptism was a public demonstration of the believer's death to the world, and being born to new life in Jesus Christ.

A central part of the baptism celebration was the public declaration of faith by each candidate. Anyone who wished to be baptised had to declare publicly his faith in Jesus Christ. At many times in the history of the Christian church, this was exceptionally dangerous: to admit to being a Christian could mean imprisonment, victimisation, suffering, or even death. (The English word 'martyr' derives from the Greek word meaning 'witness'. To be a martyr was seen as the finest witness possible to Jesus Christ and his gospel.) The believer did not, however, merely recite the creed; he was also asked, as an individual, whether he *personally* believed in the gospel, before he could be baptised. Here is part of a sermon preached in the fourth century to those who had just been baptised, in which this practice is described. (Incidentally, note the important references to Romans 6:3–4; those who have died to their past have risen to new life in Christ).

You were asked, 'Do you believe in God the father almighty?' You replied, 'I believe,' and were immersed, that is, were buried. Again, you were asked, 'Do you believe in our Lord Jesus Christ and his cross?' You replied, 'I believe,' and were immersed. Thus you were buried with Christ, for he who is buried with Christ rises again with him. A third time you were asked, 'Do you believe in the Holy Spirit?' You replied, 'I believe,' and were immersed for a third time. Your three-fold confession thus wiped out the many sins of your previous existence.

Historically, then, the Apostles' Creed was the profession of faith made by converts at their baptism, and formed the basis of their instruction. As more and more individuals now come to discover Christianity as adults, the Apostles' Creed can once more serve this historic purpose. Since then, it has served other purposes – for example, as a test of orthodoxy for Christian leaders, or as an act of praise in Christian worship. In our own day and age, the creed serves three main purposes.

In the first place, the creed provides *a brief summary of the main doctrines of the Christian faith*. A creed is not, and was never meant to be, a substitute for personal faith: it attempts to give substance to a personal faith which already exists. You do not become a Christian by reciting the creed; rather, the creed provides a useful summary of the main doctrinal points of your faith. There are certain items which are not dealt with. For example, there is no section which states 'I believe in Scripture'. This is not strictly necessary, in that the doctrines of the creed are basically a distillation or summary of the main points of the scriptural teaching concerning the gospel. The importance of Scripture is assumed throughout; indeed, most of the creed can be shown to consist of direct quotations from Scripture.

In the second place, the creed allows us to *recognise and avoid inadequate or incomplete versions of Christianity*. Some might insist that Christianity is mainly (or perhaps even entirely) about the Holy Spirit. Others might be alarmed by this, replying that Christianity is primarily about God the Father. A further group might maintain that the gospel centres upon Jesus Christ himself. The creed reminds us that there is actually much more to the gospel than any of these on their own. By providing a balanced and biblical approach to the doctrines of the Christian faith, the creed allows us to recognise deficient versions of the gospel. Many people have found their faith immeasurably strengthened and matured by being forced to think through areas of faith which they would otherwise not have explored. See the creed as an invitation to explore and discover areas of the gospel which otherwise you might miss or overlook.

Many people who have come to faith recently want to be baptised, in order to make a public declaration of their faith. A central part of that celebration of your new birth will probably be the congregation declaring their corporate faith, using the words of the creed. Let that be a stimulus to you! See the creed as setting the agenda for your personal exploration of the doctrines of the Christian faith. See it as mapping out areas for you to explore, on your own or with others. Some of its statements may remind you of those ancient maps, where vast areas of the world were marked as *terrae incognitae*, 'unknown territory'. But see this as a challenge! It may take you some time to fathom the depths of your faith; nevertheless, the result is well worth the time and effort.

In the third place, the creed emphasises a point noted earlier (chapter 5), that *to believe is to belong*. To become a Christian is to enter a community of faith, which stretches right back to the upper room (John 17:20–21). By putting your faith in Jesus Christ, you have become a member of his body, the church, which uses this creed to express its faith. By accepting and studying its doctrines, you are reminding yourself of the many men and women who have used it before you. It gives you a sense of history and perspective. It emphasises that you are not the only person to put your trust in Jesus Christ. It draws attention to the fact that its doctrines unite you with Christians down the ages and throughout the world. Think of how many others recited those words at their baptism down the centuries. Think of how many others found in the doctrines of the creed a superb statement of their personal faith. You share that faith and those doctrines, and you can share the same words that they used to express it.

USING THE CREEDS

The creeds provide an outstanding opportunity for wrestling with individual Christian doctrines, and thinking through their importance. In particular, it is helpful to ask the following questions:

1. What scriptural passages does the doctrine integrate?
2. What does it tell us about God? Jesus Christ? ourselves?
3. How can we apply it to our Christian living?
4. How does belief in this doctrine distinguish us from non-Christians?

Grappling with the doctrines of the creed is thus an excellent way of deepening our understanding of the Christian faith, and seeing how its various aspects relate. It invites us to consider the foundations of doctrine in Scripture, the manner in which it affects the way in which we live and think, and marks us off from non-Christians around us. It is an excellent subject for a study group, at an elementary or advanced level, allowing contributors to pool their ideas and insights, in order that all may come away enlightened and stimulated.

In order to encourage this process of engagement with the creeds, a worked example will be given. A relatively obscure section of the creed will serve our purposes well: 'He [Jesus Christ] suffered under Pontius Pilate.' In what follows, we shall consider the doctrinal implications of this statement of the creed, using the four questions noted above as a framework for discussion. Unfortunately, there is only space to give some samples of what might be said about this section of the creed; what follows is intended to illustrate the sort of wrestling with matters of Christian doctrine that the creed allows.

1. What biblical passages does it integrate?

A number of key passages, centering upon the passion of Christ, should be noted: Matthew 27:11–26. John 19:1–16. Note the way in which the gospel is firmly anchored to history: Pontius Pilate was a real historical individual. There are also a number of passages, scattered throughout the Epistles, which affirm that Jesus suffered, before explaining the relevance of this for believers: Romans 8:17; Hebrews 2:9, 18; 1 Peter 2:21.

2. What insights does it allow?

First and foremost, it stresses the humanity of Jesus Christ. He really did suffer, as we suffer. The New Testament stresses the humanity of Christ in other ways – for example, by noting that he became tired (John 4:6) and wept when deeply moved (John 11:35). Here is no divine figure taking on human form externally, as one might put on a coat – here is someone who really is human, who shares the experiences of our human life.

Second, the fact that he suffered under Pilate points to the tragic rejection of Jesus Christ by his world – a major theme of the New Testament. The disowning of Jesus is seen as representing the rejection of the creator by his creation. The New Testament portrays that rejection in many ways: Jesus is rejected by those who had known him from his youth at Nazareth (Luke 4:16–30). He was condemned as a blasphemer by the leaders of the Jewish people (Matt. 26:59–66).

Third, it points to the mysterious link between suffering and salvation. Jesus had to suffer in order that we might be redeemed. The doctrine of the atonement serves to remind us of the reality of sin, and the power and purpose of God to deal with it. The close relation between suffering and redemption is clearly brought out in Isaiah 52:13–53:12. This powerful and moving passage describes a mysterious suffering servant. He was innocent; he suffered on behalf of the guilty. Through his sufferings, others will be healed:

> He was despised and rejected by men, a man of sorrows and familiar with suffering . . . Surely he took up our infirmities and carried our sorrows, yet we considered him stricken by God, smitten by him and afflicted. But he was pierced for our transgressions, he was crushed for our iniquities; the punishment that brought us peace was upon him, and by his wounds we are healed. We all, like sheep, have gone astray, each of us has turned to his own way; and the Lord has laid on him the iniquity of us all . . . For he bore the sin of many, and made intercession for the transgressors.

The New Testament writers saw this passage fulfilled in the suffering of Jesus Christ (see 1 Pet. 2:21–5). His sufferings on the cross were not pointless or accidental, but the mysterious and wonderful way in which God was working out the salvation of the world. In this terse statement of the creed lie the beginnings of a doctrine of redemption.

3. How can we apply it to our Christian living?

One point may be made. Christianity has always held that it is the suffering of Christ upon the cross which is the culmination and fulfilment of his ministry. Here is the incarnate God suffering alongside us and for us. In the suffering of Jesus Christ, God shares in the darkest moments of his people. God can be found in suffering. There is a famous saying about the medical profession worth remembering here: 'Only the wounded physician can heal.' The God who offers to heal the wounds of our sin has himself been wounded by sinners.

The suffering of Jesus Christ upon the cross at Calvary does not explain suffering. It does, however, reveal that God himself is willing and able to allow himself to be subject to all the pain and suffering which his creation experiences. We are not talking of a God who stands far off from his world, aloof and distant from its problems. We are dealing with a loving God who has entered into our human situation, who became man and dwelt among us as one of us. We know a God who, in his love for us, determined to experience at first hand what it is like to be frail, mortal and human, to suffer and to die.

We cannot explain suffering, but we can say that, in the person of his Son Jesus Christ, God took it upon himself to follow this way. God became the man of suffering, so that we can enter into the mystery of death and resurrection. This is a deeply comforting thought to those who are suffering. It speaks to them of a God who knows what they are going through, who can sympathise with them. God understands their situation, and their anguish. He has been through it himself. And seen in this light, suffering assumes a new meaning. This brief statement of the creed, when fully explored, opens up a new perspective on one of the darkest sides of human life – and brings hope through the comfort of knowing that God has been through it as well.

4. How does this belief distinguish us from non-Christians?

Suffering is a mystery for everyone. It seems to serve no purpose. It denies human ability to control our situation. It is deeply threatening. The non-Christian has little to say in the face of human suffering. Socrates may have taught us how to die with dignity; Jesus Christ enables us to die in hope. The suffering of Jesus Christ allows Christians to take an attitude towards suffering which marks them off from others. Four main answers have been given to the mystery of suffering in the history of the world. First, suffering is an illusion. It is not really there, but is a product of our imaginations. Once this has been recognised, it can be dismissed. Second, suffering is real, but ends with death, leading to final peace. Third, suffering is real – but we ought to be able to rise above it, and recognise that it is of little importance. We are asked to maintain a stiff upper lip in the face of suffering, and not allow it to gain the upper hand. The Christian has the fourth, and very different, answer: God suffered in Christ. God knows what it is like to suffer. The letter to the Hebrews talks about Jesus being our 'sympathetic High Priest' (Heb. 4:15) – someone who suffers along with us (which is the literal meaning of both the Greek word *sympathetic* and the Latin word *compassionate*). This thought does not explain suffering, although it may make it more tolerable to endure. For it is expressing the deep insight that God himself suffered at first hand as we suffer. We are thus given a new perspective on life, which marks us off from the world.

There is much more that could be said. But this is intended to illustrate how useful the creeds can be in helping individuals and study groups to wrestle with matters of doctrine. See the creeds as an invitation to wrestle with the richness of the Christian faith. See them as an opportunity to explore some of its less familiar aspects. To wrestle with the doctrines of the creeds is to probe deeper into the Christian faith, and discover how rich and deep it really is.

To help individuals and study groups to wrestle more closely with some central matters of doctrine, the final part of this work will examine three key doctrines in some detail – the doctrine of the person of Jesus Christ (often referred to as the doctrine of the incarnation), the doctrine of the work of Jesus Christ (sometimes referred to as the doctrine of the atonement), and the doctrine of the Trinity. Each of these doctrines deals with central insights of the Christian faith, and they are ideally suited to the needs of those wishing to deepen their grasp of their faith.

Part III

Some Key Doctrines Examined

11 THE PERSON OF JESUS CHRIST

The Christian doctrine of the person of Jesus Christ is often discussed in terms of 'incarnation'. 'Incarnation' is a difficult yet important word, summarising the basic Christian belief that Jesus Christ is both God and man. Time after time, the New Testament represents Christ as acting as and for God in every area of crucial relevance to Christianity. When we worship Jesus Christ, we worship God; when we know Christ, we know God; when we hear the promises of Christ, we hear the promises of God; when we encounter the risen Christ, we encounter none other than the living God. The idea of the incarnation is the climax of Christian reflection upon the mystery of Christ – the recognition that Jesus Christ reveals God; that he represents God; that he speaks as God and for God; that he acts as God and for God; that he is God. In short, we must, in the words of a first-century writer, learn to 'think about Jesus as we do about God' (2 Clement 1.1–2). We are thus in a position to take the crucial step which underlies all Christian thinking on the incarnation – to say that, as Jesus Christ acts as God and for God in every context of importance, we should conclude that, for all intents and purposes, he is God.

Far from being an optional extra, something which had accidentally been added and which now requires removal, this doctrine is an essential and integral part of the authentically Christian understanding of reality. But some modern writers (such as the radical English religious critic, Don Cupitt) have laid down two fundamental challenges to this

view. First, they say, it is *wrong*. Our growing understanding
of the background to the New Testament, the way in which
Christian doctrine has developed, the rise of the scientific
world-view, and so on, force us to abandon the idea that
Jesus Christ was God in any meaningful sense of the word.
Second, they argue, it is *unnecessary*. Christianity can get on
perfectly well without the need for such obsolete and cum-
bersome ideas as God becoming man, traditionally grounded
in the resurrection of Jesus Christ and expressed in the
doctrine of the incarnation. In a world come of age, Cupitt
suggests, Christianity must learn to abandon these ideas as
archaic and irrelevant if it is to survive. In fact, however,
it seems to this writer that just about the only way in which
Christianity is likely to survive in the future is by reclaiming
its incarnational heritage as the only proper and legitimate
interpretation of the significance of Jesus Christ.

Many recent criticisms of the incarnation, such as those
expressed in the classic work of English radical religious
thought, *The Myth of God Incarnate* (1977), demonstrate a
tendency to concentrate upon objections to the *idea* of incarnation, rather than the *basis* of the idea itself. After all, the
idea of God incarnate in a specific historical human being was
quite startling within its first-century Jewish context, whatever may have been made of it in the later patristic period,
and the question of what caused this belief to arise requires
careful examination. Of central importance to this question
is the resurrection itself, a subject studiously ignored (along
with the major contributions to the incarnational discussion
by Pannenberg, Moltmann, Rahner, Kasper and others) by
most of the contributors to *The Myth of God Incarnate*.
The idea of incarnation is easy to criticise: it is paradoxical,
enigmatic, and so on. But everyone already knows this,
including the most fervent advocates of the idea! And it
is simply absurd, even to the point of being offensive, to
suggest that those who regard the incarnation as legitimate
and proper are mentally deficient, intellectually hidebound
or trapped in their traditions, unable to think for themselves.

The question remains, as it always has been: is the incarnation a proper and legitimate interpretation of the history of Jesus of Nazareth? Objections to the doctrine have tended to centre on its alleged illogicality: how can one person be two things – God and man – at one and the same time?

THE INCARNATION AS ILLOGICAL?

A serious charge against the principle of the incarnation is developed by the radical theologian John Hick who asserts ('argues' is hardly an appropriate word to use, given Hick's style of writing) that the idea of Christ being both God and man is logically contradictory. Quoting Spinoza, Hick asserts that talk of one who is both God and man is like talking about a square circle. Hick's sensitivity at this point is difficult to follow, as he is already committed to the belief that all the concepts of God to be found in the world religions – personal and impersonal, immanent and transcendent – are compatible with each other. Indeed, such is the variety of the concepts of divinity currently in circulation in the world religions that Hick seems to be obliged to turn a blind eye to the resulting logical inconsistency between them – only to seize upon and censure this alleged 'inconsistency' in the case of the incarnation. But Hick cannot be allowed to make unchallenged this robust assertion concerning the logical incompatibility of God and man, and his less than adequate knowledge of the development of Christology in the medieval period is clearly demonstrated in this matter. The fact that there is no *logical* incompatibility between God and man in the incarnation was demonstrated, and then theologically exploited, by that most brilliant of all English theologians, William of Ockham, in the fourteenth century. Ockham's discussion of this point is exhaustive and highly influential, and has yet to be discredited.

More seriously, Hick seems to work on the basis of the assumption that we know *exactly* what God is like, and on the basis of this knowledge are in a position to pass judgement on the logical niceties of the incarnation. But this is obviously not the case! Hick may be saying that there is a logical problem involved with classical theism (a *philosophical* system) in relation to the incarnation – but this is merely to suggest that classical theism is not necessarily compatible with Christianity, a point which has been made with increasing force by theologians such as Jürgen Moltmann and Eberhard Jüngel in recent years. It is not to discredit the incarnation! Hick may be in a position to say that God is totally unable to come amongst us as a human being, and that the incarnation is impossible on account of who and what God is – but if he can do so, he would seem to have access to a private and infallible knowledge of God denied to the rest of us! And do we really fully understand what is meant by that deceptively familiar word 'man'? Do we really have a total and exhaustive grasp of what it is to be human? Many of us would prefer to say that the incarnation discloses the true nature of divinity and humanity, rather than approaching the incarnation on the basis of preconceived ideas of divinity and humanity.

The fact that something is paradoxical and even self-contradictory does not invalidate it, as many critics of the incarnation seem to think. Those of us who have worked in the scientific field are only too aware of the sheer complexity and mysteriousness of reality. The events lying behind the rise of quantum theory, the difficulties of using models in scientific explanation – to name but two factors which I can remember particularly clearly from my own period as a natural scientist – point to the inevitability of paradox and contradiction in any except the most superficial engagement with reality. Our apprehension of reality is partial and fragmentary, whether we are dealing with our knowledge of the natural world or of God. The Enlightenment world-view tended to suppose that reality could be totally apprehended in rational terms, an assumption which still persists in some theological circles, even where it has been abandoned as unrealistic elsewhere. All too many modern theologians cry

'Contradiction!', and expect us all to abandon whatever it is that is supposed to be contradictory there and then. But reality just isn't like that.

We have sketched one of the most important objections raised recently against the doctrine of the incarnation of Jesus Christ, and indicated briefly the way in which it can be met. It has not been possible to do justice to this objection or the responses to it, and all that we have had the opportunity to do is to note how resurrection and incarnation alike are 'bloodied but unbowed' through recent criticisms. But one final point may be made before moving on. All too often, we are given the impression that something dramatic has happened recently, which suddenly forces everyone of any intellectual respectability to abandon faith in these matters. We are told that in a world come of age, ideas such as resurrection and incarnation are to be discarded as pre-modern, perhaps as vestiges of a cultic idol. We are children of the modern period, and must abandon the doctrinal heritage of the past. Many critics of the doctrine of the incarnation appear to envisage their criticisms as establishing a new, more relevant and universal version of Christianity.

But what might this new version of Christianity be like? The inclusion of the word 'new' is deliberate and weighed: historically, Christianity has regarded the doctrines of the resurrection and incarnation as essential to its identity, and any attempt to eliminate or radically modify them would seem to lead to a version of Christianity which is not continuous with the historical forms it has taken in the course of its development. In the following section, we shall look at the result of the elimination or radical modification of these two traditional ideas.

THE INCARNATION AND THE LOVE OF GOD

On the basis of a number of important works reflecting the spirit of Enlightenment modernism, it is clear that a central idea congenial to the modern spirit is that Christ reveals to us the love of God. It is frequently pointed out that the modern age is able to dispense with superstitious ideas about the death of Christ (for example, that it represented a victory over Satan or the payment of a legal penalty of some sort), and instead get to the real meat of the New Testament, so movingly expressed in the parable of the Prodigal Son, and modern Christianity – the love of God for humanity. In what follows, I propose to suggest that abandoning the ideas of resurrection and the incarnation means abandoning even this tender insight.

This may seem an outrageous suggestion to make, but I cannot see how this conclusion can be avoided. How may the death of Jesus Christ upon a cross at Calvary be interpreted as a demonstration of the love of God for humanity? Remember, the idea that Jesus Christ *is* God cannot be permitted, given the presuppositions of modernism. Once modernism dispenses with the idea of incarnation, a number of possible alternative explanations of the cross remain open.

1. It represented the devastating and unexpected end to the career of Jesus, forcing his disciples to invent the idea of the resurrection to cover up the totality of this catastrophe.
2. It represents God's judgement upon the career of Jesus, demonstrating that he was cursed by the Law of Moses, and thus disqualified from any putative messianic status.
3. It represents the inevitable fate of anyone who attempts to lead a life of obedience to God.
4. It represents the greatest love which one human being can show for another (cf. John 15:13) inspiring Jesus' followers to demonstrate an equal love for others.
5. The cross demonstrates that God is a sadistic tyrant.
6. The cross is meaningless.

All of these are plausible, within the framework of modernism. The idea that the cross demonstrates the love of God for man cannot, however, be included among this list. It is not *God* who is dying upon the cross, who gives himself for his people. It is a man – an especially splendid man, who may be ranked with others in history who have made equally great sacrifices for those whom they loved. The death of an innocent person at the hands of corrupt judges is all too common, even today, and Jesus Christ cannot be singled out for special discussion unless he *is* something or someone qualitatively different from us.

A critic might, of course, immediately reply that Jesus Christ is a higher example of the kind of inspiration or illumination to be found in all human beings, so that he must be regarded as the outstanding human being – and for that reason, his death assumes an especial significance. But this is a remarkably dogmatic assumption – that Jesus Christ is unique among human beings in this respect! The uniqueness of Christ was established by the New Testament writers through the resurrection (Rom. 1:3–4) and the subsequent recognition that Christ was none other than the living God dwelling among us. But this insight is given and guaranteed by two doctrines which some radical modern writers cannot allow – the resurrection and incarnation. It would seem that modernists are prepared to retain insights gained through the traditional framework of resurrection and incarnation – and then declare that this framework may be dispensed with. It is as if the traditional framework is treated as some sort of learning aid, which may be dispensed with once the ideas in question are mastered.

But this is clearly questionable, to say the least. If the traditional framework is declared to be wrong, the consequences of this declaration for each and every aspect of Christian theology must be ascertained. Discard or radically modify the doctrines of resurrection and incarnation, and the idea of the 'uniqueness' or the 'superiority' of Christ becomes a dogmatic assertion without foundation, an assertion which many of more humanist inclinations would find offensive. We would be equally justified in appealing to other historical figures – such as Socrates or Gandhi – as encapsulating the desiderata of Christian moral behaviour.

This point becomes more important when we return to the question of how the death of Christ can be interpreted as a self-giving divine act, demonstrating the love of God for humanity. It is not God who is upon the cross: it is a human being. That point must be conceded by those who reject the incarnation. It may then be the case that God makes his love known indirectly (and, it must be said, in a remarkably ambiguous manner) through the death of Jesus Christ, but we have lost for ever the insight that it is God himself who shows his love for us on the cross. What the cross might conceivably demonstrate, among a number of other, more probable, possibilities, is the full extent of the love of one human being for others. And as the love of human beings can be thought of as mirroring the love of God, it would therefore be taken as an indirect demonstration of what the love of God is like, in much the same way that countless other individuals throughout history have given up their lives to save their friends or families. But who did Christ die to save? None, save possibly Barabbas, can be said to have benefited directly from his death, and it would seem that modernism would like us to understand Christ's death as making some sort of religious point which will enrich our spiritual lives. But this is not how the New Testament writers understood his death (not least because they insisted upon interpreting that death in the light of the resurrection, a procedure regarded as illegitimate by modernists), and it is certainly difficult to see how it would have cut much ice in the hostile environment in which Christianity had to survive and expand in the first period of its existence.

The traditional framework for discussion of the revelation of the love of God in the death of Christ is that of God humbling himself and coming among us as one of us, taking upon himself the frailty and mortality of our human nature in order to redeem it. To deny that the lonely dying figure upon the cross is God is to lose this point of contact, and to return to the view which Christianity overturned in its own day and age – that 'God is with us only in his transcendence' (Don Cupitt). A divine representative – not God himself – engages with the pain and suffering of this world. It is his love, not God's, which is shown. And to those who might think that this difficulty may be eliminated by developing the idea of God allowing himself to be identified with the dying Christ, it may be pointed out that the exploration of this idea by Moltmann and Jüngel leads not merely to an incarnational, but to a *Trinitarian*, theology. In order to do justice to the Christian experience of God through Jesus Christ, a higher profile of identification between Christ and God than function is required – we are dealing with an identity of being, rather than just an identification of function. Jesus Christ acts as and for God precisely because he *is* God.

THE INCARNATION AND SUFFERING

A similar point may be made in relation to suffering. Twentieth-century apologetics has recognised that any theology which is unable to implicate God in some manner in the sufferings and pain of the world condemns itself as inadequate and deficient. The twentieth century witnessed previously unimagined horrors of human suffering in the trenches of the First World War, in the extermination camps of Nazi Germany, and the programmes of genocide established by Nazi Germany and Marxist Cambodia. The rise of 'protest atheism' – perhaps one of the most powerful sentiments to which modern theology must address itself – reflects human moral revulsion at these acts. Protest atheism has a tendency to select soft targets, and there are few targets softer in this respect than a non-incarnational theology.

   An incarnational theology speaks of God subjecting himself to the evil and pain of the world at its worst, in the grim scene at Calvary, bearing the brunt of that agony itself. God suffered in Christ, taking upon himself the suffering and pain of the world which he created. In her essay 'Creed or Chaos' (1940), Dorothy L. Sayers wrote:

> It is only with the confident assertion of the creative divinity of the Son that the doctrine of the Incarnation becomes a real revelation of the structure of the world. And here Christianity has its enormous advantage over every other religion in the world. It is the *only* religion which gives value to evil and suffering. It affirms – not, like Christian Science, that evil has no real existence, nor yet, like Buddhism, that good consists in a refusal to experience evil – but that perfection is attained through the active and positive effort to wrench a real good out of a real evil.

A non-incarnational theology is forced, perhaps against its basic instincts, to speak of a God who may send his condolences through a representative, but who does not (or cannot, for fear of being accused of logical contradiction?) enter into and share his people's suffering at first hand. And for a modernist, highly critical of substitutionary theories of the atonement, God can hardly be allowed to take responsibility for the suffering of the world vicariously, through a human representative, who suffers instead of and on behalf of God. In 1963, the English *Sunday Observer* publicised John Robinson's book *Honest to God* with the headline 'Our image of God must go'. The image that Robinson had in mind was that of an old man in the sky. But the 'image of God that must go' in the face of the intense and deadly serious moral criticisms of protest atheism is that of a God who does not experience human suffering and pain at first hand – in short, a non-incarnational image of God. Many of those who criticise the incarnation seem to realise the force of this point, and attempt to retain it, despite their intellectual misgivings. Perhaps in the end, it will not be the protests of orthodoxy which destroy non-incarnational theologies, but protest atheism, which wisely and rightly detects the fundamental weakness of such a theology in precisely this respect.

THE INCARNATION AND REDEMPTION

A further vital consideration concerns the whole doctrine of redemption, the fulcrum of the Christian faith. If God has not redeemed us through Jesus Christ, the entire gospel is false, and the Christian hope little more than a cruel illusion. The electrifying declaration that God has redeemed us through Jesus Christ has as its central presupposition that he *is* God. This point was made with great force by the third-century writer Athanasius, who argued along the following lines.

Athanasius insists that it is only God who can save. God, and God alone, can break the power of sin, and bring us to eternal life. In doing this, Athanasius takes up a great Old Testament tradition (see, for example, Isa. 45:21–2). There is no point in looking to horses, armies, princes or any worldly authorities for salvation: God alone can save. Athanasius builds his argument on this important premise. No creature can save another creature – only the creator can redeem his creation.

Having emphasised that it is God alone who can save, Athanasius then makes the logical move which Arius found difficult to counter. The New Testament regards Jesus Christ as the proper saviour of humanity. New Testament texts making this suggestion would include Matthew 1:21 (which speaks of Jesus saving his people from their sins), Luke 2:11 (the famous Christmas message of the angels: 'Today in the town of David a Saviour has been born to you'), Acts 4:12 (which affirms that salvation comes through Jesus), Hebrews 2:10 (which calls Jesus the 'author of salvation'). According to the New Testament, it is *Jesus* who is the Saviour. Yet, as Athanasius emphasised, only God can save. So how are we to make sense of this?

The only possible solution, Athanasius argues, is to accept that Jesus is God incarnate. The logic of his argument goes something like this:

Only God can save.
Jesus saves.
Therefore Jesus is God.

This sort of logic seems to underlie some New Testament passages. For example, Titus 1:3–4 speaks of 'God our saviour' at one point, and 'Christ Jesus our Saviour' at another. Now Athanasius is able to strengthen his argument by pointing out that no creature can save another creature. Salvation involves divine intervention. Athanasius thus draws out the meaning of John 1:14 by arguing that the 'word became flesh': in other words, God entered into our human situation, in order to change it. To use Athanasius' own words: 'God became man so that we might become God.' If Jesus Christ was just a creature like the rest of us, he would be part of the problem, rather than its solution. He would share our dilemma, rather than being able to liberate us from it.

THE INCARNATION AND THE SIGNIFICANCE OF JESUS CHRIST

A final point which may be made concerns the permanent significance of Jesus Christ. Why is he of such importance to the Christian faith here and now, some twenty centuries after his death? The traditional answer is that his significance lay in his being God incarnate; that in his specific historical existence, God assumed human nature. All else is secondary to this central insight, deriving from reflection upon the significance of his resurrection. The fact that Jesus was male; the fact that he was a Jew; the precise nature of his teaching – all these are secondary to the fact that God took upon himself human nature, thereby lending it new dignity and meaning.

But if Jesus Christ is not God incarnate, his significance

must be evaluated in terms of those parameters which traditional Christianity has treated as secondary or accidental (in the Aristotelian sense of the term). Immediately, we are confronted with the problem of historical conditioning: what conceivable relevance may the teachings and lifestyle of a first-century male Jew have for us today, in a totally different cultural situation? The maleness of Christ has caused offence in radical feminist circles: why should women be forced to relate to a male religious teacher, whose teaching may be compromised by his very masculinity, as well as by the patriarchal values of his cultural situation? And why should modern western humanity pay any attention to the culturally-conditioned teaching of such an individual, given the seemingly insuperable cultural chasm dividing first-century Palestine and the twentieth-century west? And even the concept of the 'religious personality' of Jesus has been seriously eroded, as much by New Testament scholarship as by shifts in cultural expectations. For reasons such as these, a non-incarnational Christianity is unable convincingly to anchor the person of Jesus Christ as the centre of the Christian faith. He may be the historical point of departure for that faith, but its subsequent development involves the leaving behind of the historical particularity of his existence in order to confront the expectations of each social milieu in which Christianity may subsequently find itself. Jesus Christ says *this* – but we say *that*. *This* may be acceptable in a first-century Palestinian context – but *that* is acceptable in a modern western culture, in which we live and move and have our being. Jesus Christ is thus both relativised and marginalised. Many non-incarnational versions of Christianity accept and welcome such insights – but others find them disturbing, and perhaps unconsciously articulate an incarnational Christianity in order to preserve insights which they intuitively recognise as central.

In this chapter, we have briefly summarised the case for defending the doctrine of the incarnation as a proper and legitimate interpretation of the history of Jesus of Nazareth, and rejecting alternative explanations as inadequate. In no way whatsoever can it be said that this matter has been discussed adequately: the volumes this demands are just not available. Nevertheless, it is hoped that the contours of the case for arguing that the doctrine of the incarnation is a proper and necessary element of the Christian faith have been sketched in sufficient detail to allow the reader to take his or her own thinking further. We end this chapter with some final reflections.

Critics of doctrines such as the incarnation tend to work on the basis of two presuppositions. First, that there exists a theological equivalent of precision surgery, which allows certain elements of the Christian faith to be excised without having any detrimental effect whatsoever upon what remains. Second, that by eliminating logical and metaphysical difficulties, a more plausible and hence more acceptable version of Christianity will result. Both these assumptions are clearly questionable, and must be challenged.

As C.S. Lewis wrote to Arthur Greaves on 11 December 1944: 'The doctrine of Christ's divinity seems to me not something stuck on which you can unstick but something that peeps out at every point so that you'd have to unravel the whole web to get rid of it.' For C.S. Lewis, the coherence of Christianity was such that it was impossible to eliminate the idea of the divinity of Christ without doing such damage to the web of Christian doctrine that the entire structure of the Christian faith would collapse.

To return to our surgical analogy, we are not talking about the removal of an appendix (a vestigial organ apparently serving no useful purpose), but of the heart, the life-pump of the Christian faith. Faith in the resurrection and incarnation is what kept and keeps Christianity growing and spreading. The sheer vitality, profundity and excitement of the Christian faith ultimately depends upon these. In a day and age when Christianity has to fight for its existence, winning converts rather than relying upon a favourable cultural milieu, a non-incarnational theology despoiled of the resurrection has little to commend it. It is perhaps significant that many critics of the resurrection and incarnation were themselves originally attracted to Christianity through precisely the theology they are now criticising. And what, it must be asked in all seriousness, is the *converting power* of an incarnationless Christianity?

The history of the church suggests that such a version of Christianity is a spiritual dead end. In the fourth century, as has been discussed, such a version of Christianity temporarily developed, associated with the writer Arius. To its critics, incarnationless Christianity seems to be scholarly, bookish and devoid of passion, without the inner dynamism to challenge and conquer unbelief in a world in which this is essential for its survival. In the characteristically pithy words of Dorothy L. Sayers: 'If Christ was only man, then he is entirely irrelevant to any thought about God; if he is only God, then he is entirely irrelevant to any experience of human life.' But this is where history will pass its own judgement, in that only a form of Christianity which is convinced that it has something distinctive, true, exciting and relevant to communicate to the world in order to transform it, will survive.

In this chapter, we have examined the doctrine of the incarnation, in order to illustrate some aspects of the nature of Christian doctrine. Even in doing so, the coherence of Christian doctrine became evident. In discussing the person of Christ (specifically, the doctrine of the incarnation), we were unable to avoid discussing its implications for the work of Christ (specifically, the demonstration of the love of God in the death of Christ). In the following chapter, we shall pursue this second area of Christian doctrine.

12 THE WORK OF JESUS CHRIST

A central area of Christian theology focuses on the question of what Jesus Christ achieved through his death and resurrection. In older textbooks, especially those written in the nineteenth century, this area of Christian doctrine is often referred to as 'the atonement'. The origins of the word 'atonement' can be traced back to 1526, when the English writer William Tyndale was confronted with the task of translating the New Testament into English. There was, at that time, no English word which meant 'reconciliation'. Tyndale thus had to invent such a word – 'at-one-ment'. This word soon came to bear the meaning 'the benefits which Jesus Christ brings to believers through his death upon the cross'. This unfamiliar word is rarely used in modern English, and has a distinctively archaic flavour to it. Rather than convey the impression that Christian thought is totally out of date, theologians now prefer to speak of this area as 'the doctrine of the work of Christ'.

Throughout the New Testament, we find stress on the fact that God has acted, has achieved something, through the death and resurrection of Jesus Christ. Something has happened through Jesus Christ, which otherwise would not and could not have taken place. The New Testament uses a wide range of images and ideas to attempt to express what it is that God has done through Christ. In an attempt to integrate the richness of the scriptural affirmations concerning the work of Jesus Christ, a number of ways of approaching this vast subject have been developed. Occasionally, these are still referred to as 'theories of the atonement,' although this expression is not especially helpful. In what follows, we shall look at the three most influential ways of approaching the meaning of the cross and resurrection. Each of these integrates a range of biblical ideas and emphases, and has considerable implications for human experience of ourselves and of God.

A VICTORY OVER SIN AND DEATH

The first way of approaching the meaning of the cross integrates a series of biblical passages focusing upon the notion of a divine victory over hostile forces. The New Testament declares that God has given us a victory through the resurrection of Jesus Christ (1 Cor. 15:57). But in what way may this victory be understood? Who is it who has been defeated? And how? The Christian writers of the first five centuries (often collectively designated 'the fathers') were captivated by the imagery of Christ gaining a victory through the cross. It was clear to them that Christ had defeated death, sin and the devil. Just as David killed Goliath with his own weapons, so Christ defeated sin with its weapon – death. Through an apparent defeat, victory was gained over a host of hidden forces which tyrannised humanity.

The fathers spelled out this tyranny, using a number of central images. We were held in bondage by the fear of death. We were imprisoned by sin. We were trapped by the power of the devil. With great skill, these writers built up a coherent picture of the human dilemma. Human beings are held prisoner by a matrix of hostile forces, and are unable to break free unaided. Someone was required who would break into their prison, and set them free. Someone from outside the human situation would have to enter into our predicament, and liberate us. Someone would have to cut the bonds which held us captive. Time and time again, the same theme is restated: we are trapped in our situation, and our only hope lies in liberation from outside.

The great and thrilling news of the Christian gospel is therefore that God has entered into the human situation in his Son, Jesus Christ. Through his death and resurrection, Christ confronted and disarmed the host of hostile forces which collectively held us in captivity. The cross and resurrection represent a dramatic act of divine liberation, in which God delivers his people from captivity to hostile powers, as he once delivered his people Israel from bondage in Egypt. The second-century writer Irenaeus of Lyons put it like this. 'The Word of God was made flesh in order that he might destroy death and bring us to life. For we were tied and bound in sin, we were born in sin, and we live under the dominion of death.'

A number of the great hymns of the medieval church make this point. For example, the hymn *Panga lingua* stresses the triumph of the cross through the paradox that its victim was actually its victor:

> Sing my tongue the glorious battle!
> Sing the ending of the fray!
> Now above the cross the trophy,
> Sound the loud triumphal lay!
> Tell how Christ the world's redeemer,
> As a victim won the day!

(Incidentally, note the importance of Christian hymns and songs as means of making doctrinal statements. The hymn books of the Christian church are often its most important and most memorable statements of doctrine.)

In dealing with this theme of Christ's victory through the apparent defeat of the cross, the fathers were especially attracted to the scriptural image of a 'ransom'. The New Testament talks about Jesus giving his life as a 'ransom' for sinners (Mark 10:45; 1 Tim. 2:6). What does this analogy mean? The everyday use of the word 'ransom' suggests three ideas.

1. *Liberation.* A ransom is something which achieves freedom for a person who is held in captivity. When someone is kidnapped, and a ransom demanded, the payment of that ransom leads to liberation.
2. *Payment.* A ransom is a sum of money which is paid in order to achieve an individual's liberation.
3. *Someone to whom the ransom is paid.* A ransom is usually paid to an individual's captor, or his agent.

These three ideas seem to be implied by speaking of Jesus' death as a 'ransom' for sinners.

The fathers thus developed the idea that the death of Jesus Christ upon the cross was a payment made to the devil, in order to persuade him to liberate humanity from its bondage to him. In extending this theory, the fathers argued that, on account of human sin, we are all subject to the power and authority of the devil. There was no way that we could break free from this serfdom. However, God provided a payment, by which the devil was induced to hand over humanity to God their creator. They were thus ransomed.

This idea will probably seem deeply disturbing to many readers. But to the fathers, it was a perfectly proper doctrine, based upon the three elements of the scriptural analogy of ransom. But are all of these three actually present in Scripture? There is no doubt whatsoever that the New Testament proclaims that we have been liberated from captivity through the death and resurrection of Jesus. We have been set free from captivity to sin and the fear of death (Rom. 8:21; Heb. 2:15). It is also clear that the New Testament understands the death of Jesus as the price which had to be paid to achieve our liberation (1 Cor. 6:20; 7:23). Our liberation is a costly and a precious matter. In these two respects, the scriptural use of 'redemption' corresponds to the everyday use of the word. But what of the third aspect?

There is not a hint in the New Testament that Jesus' death was the price paid to someone (such as the devil) to achieve our liberation. Some of the writers of the first five centuries, however, assumed that they could press this analogy to its limits, and declared that God had delivered us from the power of the devil by offering him Jesus as the price of our liberation. But this idea is without scriptural warrant, and actually amounts to a serious distortion of the New Testament understanding of the meaning of the death of Jesus Christ. It is therefore important to consider how far we are allowed to press analogies before they break down, and mislead us.

The idea of Christ's death and resurrection as a victory over hidden forces which oppress us continues to be enormously helpful to many Christians. Many African Christians, for example, find it very helpful to think of the cross and resurrection of Jesus Christ as breaking the baleful influence of malevolent ancestors and evil spirits upon their lives. The Second World War in Europe also brought new relevance to the idea, and also allowed new insights to be gained concerning the Christian life. One central question thus illuminated is the following: If Christ gained a victory over sin, why do Christians still experience a continuing conflict with sin in their lives?

In his work *Christ and Time*, the distinguished New Testament scholar Oscar Cullmann showed how events of the Second World War cast light upon the great scriptural theme of the victory of Christ over sin, and also addressed the question just noted. Cullmann suggested that it was helpful to think of a pattern of events which the war had made only too familiar to many Europeans: a long period of occupation by a foreign power. A country is occupied by an invading force, and its people held captive. There is no hope of liberation from within. A sense of despondency and hopelessness begins to creep in.

Then the situation is dramatically altered. Liberating forces establish a bridgehead on occupied territory. A great battle is won, and the course of the war is irreversibly altered. Yet the battle goes on. It is only when the last of the foreign forces have been defeated that victory is finally complete.

(Cullmann has in mind the events of D-Day, which gave Allied forces a foothold in occupied Europe, and VE-Day, when the German armies finally surrendered.) Looking back on events from after VE-Day, it is clear that the war entered a decisive new phase at D-Day. Victory was given with that strategic struggle. And yet, in another sense, victory was not given, in that the war in Europe would continue for the best part of another year. But the will of the Nazi armies to resist had been broken at that decisive moment.

Similarly, the cross and resurrection represent a decisive battle, in which God confronts the age-old enemies of humanity through the cross of Christ. Their power is broken. They are defeated. Yet they have yet to be utterly conquered. Mopping-up operations must go on. The power of sin over us may be broken, but it continues to fight a rearguard action, however hopeless. The doctrine of the work of Christ assures us of final victory over sin and death, despite the fact that they are still at work in the world around us.

A PENALTY FOR HUMAN SIN

A second approach to the meaning of the death of Christ integrates a series of biblical passages dealing with notions of judgement and forgiveness. The understanding of the work of Christ outlined above has enormous attractions, not least on account of its highly dramatic character. It also, however, has some serious weaknesses. For the eleventh-century writer Anselm of Canterbury, two weaknesses were of particular importance. In the first place, it failed to explain why God should wish to redeem us. And, in the second, it was of little value in understanding how Jesus Christ was involved in the process of redemption. Anselm felt that more explanation was required.

To meet this need, he developed an approach to the work of Christ which centres upon the rectitude of the created order. God created the world in a certain way, which expresses his divine nature. He also created human beings in order that they might have fellowship in eternity with him. This purpose, however, would seem to have been frustrated by human sin, which comes as a barrier between us and God. A fundamental disruption has been introduced into creation. Its moral ordering has been violated. The redemption of humanity is thus called for, in order that the natural rectitude of the created order may be restored. In this sense, Anselm understands redemption as a restoration of humanity to its original status within creation.

How, then, can we be redeemed? Anselm stresses that God is obliged to redeem us in a way that is consistent with the moral ordering of the creation, reflecting the nature of God himself. God cannot create the universe in one way, as an expression of his will and nature, and then violate its moral order in the redemption of humanity. He must redeem us in a way that is consistent with his own nature and purposes. Redemption must be moral, and be seen to be moral. God cannot employ one standard of morality at one point, and another later on. He is therefore under a self-imposed obligation to respect the moral order of the creation. His personal integrity demands that he be faithful to his own moral principles in redeeming us (see pp. 81–3).

Having established this point forcefully, Anselm then considers how redemption is possible. The basic dilemma can be summarised as follows. God cannot restore us to fellowship with him, without first dealing with human sin. Sin is a disruption of the moral ordering of the universe. It represents the rebellion of the creation against its creator. It represents an insult and an offence to God. The situation must be made right before fellowship can be restored. God must 'make good' the situation. Anselm thus introduces the concept of a 'satisfaction' – a payment or other action which compensates for the offence of human sin. Once this satisfaction has been made, the situation can revert to normal. But this satisfaction *must* be made first.

The problem, Anselm then observes, is that human beings do not have the ability to make this satisfaction. It lies beyond their resources. They need to make it – but cannot. Anselm thus reaches a crucial stage in his argument. Humanity ought to make satisfaction for its sins, but cannot. God himself is under no obligation to make satisfaction – but he could, if he wanted to. Therefore, Anselm argues, if God were to become a man, the resulting God-man would have both the obligation (as man) and the ability (as God) to make satisfaction. Thus the incarnation leads to a just solution to the human dilemma. God can redeem us, while maintaining his personal integrity. The death of Jesus Christ upon the cross demonstrates God's total opposition to sin, while at the same time providing the means by which sin could be really and truly forgiven, and the way opened to renewed fellowship between humanity and God.

But how does Christ's achievement upon the cross affect us? In what way do we share in the benefits of his death and resurrection? Anselm felt that this point did not require discussion, and so gave no guidance on the matter. Later writers, however, felt that it needed to be addressed. Three main ways of understanding how believers relate to Christ in this manner may be noted.

1. Participation

Through faith, believers participate in Jesus Christ. They are 'in Christ', to use Paul's famous phrase. They are caught up in him, and share in his risen life. As a result of this, they share in all the benefits won by Christ, through his obedience upon the cross.

2. Representation

Christ is the covenant representative of humanity. Through faith, we come to stand within the covenant between God and humanity. All that Christ has won for us is available to us, on account of the covenant. Just as God entered into a covenant with his people Israel, so he has entered into a covenant with his church. Christ, by his obedience upon the cross, represents his covenant people, winning benefits for them as their representative. By coming to faith, individuals come to stand within the covenant, and thus participate in all its benefits, won by Christ.

3. Substitution

Christ is here understood to be our substitute. We ought to have been crucified, on account of our sins; Christ is crucified in our place. God allows Christ to stand in our place, taking his guilt upon himself, in order that his righteousness – won by obedience upon the cross – might become ours.

Each of these three approaches has merits in explaining how the believer comes to benefit from the death and resurrection of Christ.

A DEMONSTRATION OF THE LOVE OF GOD

If these two accounts of the meaning and inner dynamic of the cross of Christ are flawed at any point, it is perhaps most obviously in their failure to do justice to the love of God. Peter Abelard, a near-contemporary of Anselm of Canterbury, gently chided him for this apparent omission. How could one speak of the cross of Christ without also wanting to speak of the love of God for us?

The third approach to the death of Christ integrates a cluster of biblical passages which relate the death of Christ to the tender love of God for sinners. The New Testament affirms that the death of Jesus Christ demonstrates the love of God for us (John 3:16; Rom. 5:8). There can be no doubt that this insight is essential to any complete and balanced Christian account of the meaning of the death of Christ. As we saw earlier, this insight is safeguarded by a cluster of doctrines – above all, that of the incarnation (pp. 139–143). We are enabled to avoid abstract and vague ways of thinking about the love of God, and can begin to say precisely what form it takes. The love of God is like the love of a man, who voluntarily lays down his life for his friends (John 15:13). In the tragic scene of Jesus trudging his lonely and painful road to the cross, there to die for those whom he loved, we are given a vivid and deeply moving picture of what the love of God is like. The commitment and pain of that love are brought home to us every time we read the passion stories of the Gospels. To realise that God loves us – and loves us so much – is a devastating insight.

There is, however, a real danger here. Salvation can be reduced simply to a change in our perception of the situation. Nothing has changed – except that we realise that God loves us. We remain sinners. We remain trapped within our sinful situation. The death of Christ is like a catalyst, or a particularly powerful learning aid, which triggers off our recognition of the fact that God loves us. Up to this point, we may have been labouring under the delusion that God is wrathful, and liable to punish sinners. From that point onwards, we rejoice in the recognition that God actually (whatever we may have thought earlier) loves us. And this insight changes our lives. We are liberated by this knowledge.

The difficulty I have with this theory is perhaps best explored with reference to the writings of Karl Marx, especially the *Economic and Philosophical Manuscripts* of 1844. In these papers, Marx considers the question of human alienation. He distinguishes two broad senses of the term: a psychological sense, in which human beings are subjectively alienated from their true being; and an economic sense, in which they are objectively alienated from their property rights. Marx argues powerfully that a subjective feeling of alienation arises from an objective state of alienation. You feel alienated because you are alienated – alienated from your proper social, political and economic rights. No amount of tinkering around with the human subjective consciousness is going to change this situation. So long as humans are socially alienated, they will continue to be psychologically alienated.

Marx thus argues that the proper way of achieving psychological tranquillity is through improvement of the social, political and economic situation of individuals and society. Marx's point can be made with reference to a common problem in modern urban society. Many people are depressed. They suffer from a psychological condition, which can be treated, at least to some extent, by psychological techniques. But if these people then have to go and live in appalling social conditions, in bad housing, under constant threat of violence, and permanently short of money, they become depressed again. There is an objective cause to their subjective state of depression.

With this analogy in mind, let us return to our discussion of the work of Jesus Christ. Our subjective feeling of alienation from God is grounded in our objective state of alienation from God. We *feel* alienated because we *are* alienated from God. It is not just as if we *think* that we are sinners; we *are* sinners. It is not just that we *think* we are cut off from God; we *are* cut off from God. Our situation must be changed. We must be brought into a new relationship with God. To think of Christ dying on the cross just to change the way we think is dangerously shallow. Rather, Christ's death upon the cross changes our situation, in both its objective and subjective aspects. We are brought into a new relationship with God, in which the threat posed by sin is neutralised. And we respond to God, in the knowledge that he loves us and that we are free to love him.

In 1915, Hastings Rashdall delivered a series of Bampton Lectures at Oxford University. In these lectures, Rashdall argued forcefully that Jesus Christ was a moral example whom we are called to imitate. Having realised that God loves us, through contemplation of the death of Christ, we are moved to echo that love within our hearts – and thus to imitate Jesus, as an expression of our love for God. There is nothing, Rashdall asserted, fundamentally wrong with human nature, except that we fail to appreciate that God loves us.

Unfortunately, there were not that many present to hear Rashdall's lectures. Most of Oxford's young men were at the front, involved in some of the worst carnage the human race has ever seen. Even as Rashdall spoke, the First World War had plumbed new depths of human depravity. It was obvious to all that there was something fundamentally wrong with human nature – an impression to be confirmed by the shocking episodes of the Second World War, such as Auschwitz. Human beings needed more than education – they needed transformation. An understanding of the cross of Christ as moral education is inadequate, precisely because it rests upon an inadequate and unrealistic view of human nature. A deficient understanding of the human predicament leads to a defective understanding of the nature of the solution offered.

Having considered these three main ways of approaching the doctrine of the work of Christ, we may briefly explore some of its implications. One of the more important aspects of the Christian doctrine of salvation is its logical implication – original sin. Christianity proclaims that Christ is the saviour of all human beings. If this is the case, then all human beings must require redemption. The presupposition of the doctrine of universal redemption of humanity through Christ is the universal sinfulness of humanity. 'All have sinned and fall short of the glory of God' (Rom. 3:23).

What does this imply about human nature? Two points may be made. First, it does not imply that God made humanity with inbuilt defects. The doctrine of the fall asserts that human nature, having been created by God, fell into sin. Sin is a consequence of the independent action of God's creatures, rather than of any defective action on the part of the creator himself. Classical Christian theology locates the origins of sin in the human desire to be God, to usurp the place of God, to play at being the creator rather than accepting the status of being a creature. Second, it allows us to draw an important distinction between *fallen* and *redeemed* human nature. Although fallen, we remain the creation of God. We are still God's, even though we have sinned against him. In the process of redemption, however, we are brought into a new relationship with God. We become the children of God, with inheritance rights. A new status results. We may be sinners – but we are forgiven sinners.

How are we to think of original sin? In practice, original sin tends to be thought of as the antithesis of salvation. In other words, the way that you understand salvation affects the way you understand original sin. If you understand salvation as forgiveness, original sin is understood as legal or moral guilt. If you understand salvation as reconciliation to God, original sin is conceived as alienation from God. If salvation is understood as liberation from hostile forces, original sin is understood as enslavement to those forces. The basic function that the doctrine serves is to define the state from which we are redeemed. Many people find this doctrine puzzling; seen in its proper context, however, it can be seen as setting the scene for the great drama of redemption, which culminates in the work of Jesus Christ.

In this chapter, we have sketched various doctrinal approaches to the meaning of the death of Jesus Christ on the cross. Each of these approaches is complementary. Each integrates a different series of biblical passages. The full depths of the biblical understanding of the death of Christ are only to be appreciated by bringing together these three approaches, and the scriptural passages upon which they are based. For the death of Christ does not just involve a divine victory over sin, death and evil – it *also* involves the gaining of real forgiveness, and the demonstration of the full extent of God's love for us.

With this point in mind, we may turn to think about how doctrines of the work of Christ relate to human experience.

The three ways of thinking about the death of Christ we
have just considered address themselves to – with a view to
transforming – three different areas of human experience.

1. The cross as victory over a fear of death

Many people are frightened of death. Contemporary exis-
tentialist philosophers point out how humans try to deny
death, try to pretend that they aren't going to die. We like
to think that death is something which happens to somebody
else. It is very difficult for us to come to terms with the fact
that our personal existence will one day be terminated. It is
a very threatening and disturbing thought. People are afraid
of death. How often has it been said that death is a forbidden
subject in the modern world?

It is here that the gospel has a decisive contribution
to make. The New Testament points to the death and
resurrection of Jesus Christ as God's victory over sin and
death (1 Cor. 15:55–6). Christ 'shared in their humanity so
that by his death he might destroy him who holds the power
of death – that is, the devil – and free those who all their lives
were held in slavery by their fear of death' (Heb. 2:14–15).
The gospel invites those who are afraid of death to look at
what God has achieved through the cross and resurrection
of Jesus. So long as human beings walk the face of this
earth, knowing that they must die, the gospel will continue
to be relevant and powerful. A feeling of fear and despair
in the face of death can be changed into a sense of hope
– *real* hope – in the light of the death and resurrection of
Christ. A fundamental human experience (the fear of death)
is addressed, in order to be transformed.

2. The cross and a feeling of guilt

Many people have a deep sense of personal inadequacy
and guilt. 'How', they may ask, 'can someone like me
ever enter into a relationship with God? After all, he is

so holy and righteous, and I am so sinful and wretched.' This is a very important question, and Christianity has a very powerful answer to give. The cross demonstrates God's determination to deal with human sin. It shows just how serious and costly a thing real forgiveness is – and reassures us that our sins really have been forgiven. God doesn't say something like, 'Never mind, let's pretend that sin doesn't exist.' Instead, God brings together in the cross of Jesus his total condemnation of sin and his tender love for the sinner. We see in the death of Jesus on the cross the full impact of human sin, the full cost of divine forgiveness, and the full extent of the love of God for sinners. God hates the sin and loves the sinner. Christ endured the cross for our sakes, and bore the full penalty for sin. As a result, sin is forgiven – really forgiven. We are able to come to God, as forgiven sinners, as men and women whose sin has been condemned and forgiven. We must learn to accept that we have been accepted by God, despite being unacceptable.

So the cross is indeed good news to those who feel that they could not possibly come to God on account of their sin or inadequacy. The gospel gloriously affirms that God has forgiven that sin, has overcome that inadequacy. The words of 1 Peter 2:24 are very helpful and important here: 'He himself bore our sins in his body on the tree, so that we might die to sins and live for righteousness; by his wounds you have been healed.' Through the great events which centred on Calvary, God has wiped out our past sin and, at enormous cost, given us a fresh start. He has smoothed out every difficulty in order that we might go forward with him into eternal life. We are able to turn our backs on our past (which is what the idea of 'repentance' basically means) in order to go forward into the future with the God who loves us. Once more, a human experience (a sense of guilt or inadequacy) is addressed, in order to be transformed into a sense of forgiveness and acceptance by God.

3. The cross and the human need for love

Many people feel lost in the immensity of the universe. We all need to feel loved, to feel that we are important to someone else. Yet at the root of the lives of many, there is a virtual absence of any meaning. President John F. Kennedy once remarked that 'modern American youth has everything – except a reason to live.' And the words of Jean-Paul Sartre express this point with force: 'Here we are, all of us, eating and drinking to preserve our precious existences – and yet there is nothing, nothing, absolutely no reason for existing.' We could even give a name to this feeling of meaninglessness – we could call it an 'existential vacuum'. But that doesn't solve the problem. We still feel lonely and lost, in a vast universe which threatens to overwhelm us.

It is this feeling of meaninglessness which is transformed through the electrifying declaration that God – the same God who created the universe – loves us. Love gives meaning to life, in that the person loved becomes special to someone, assumes a significance which he otherwise might not have. Christianity makes the astonishing assertion – which it bases upon the life, death and resurrection of Jesus Christ – that God is profoundly interested in us and concerned for us. We mean something to God; Christ died for us; we are special in the sight of God. Christ came to bring us back from the 'far country' to our loving and waiting father. In the midst of an immense and frightening universe, we are given meaning and significance by the realisation that the God who called the world into being, who created us, also loves us and cares for us, coming down from heaven and going to the cross to prove the full extent of that love to a disbelieving and wondering world. Once more, a human experience (a sense of loneliness and meaninglessness) is addressed, and transformed into a sense of being dearly loved and given a sense of purpose.

The doctrine of the work of Christ, in addition to being an important area of Christian thought in its own right, is also of significance in that it illustrates the manner in which doctrine seeks to integrate Scripture and interpret and transform experience. Much the same is true of the doctrine of the Trinity, to which we now turn.

13 THE TRINITY

For many Christians, the doctrine of the Trinity is perhaps one of the most obscure aspects of Christian theology. Many read the puzzling words of the Athanasian Creed – 'The Father incomprehensible, the Son incomprehensible, and the Holy Spirit incomprehensible' – and feel sorely tempted to add, 'the whole thing incomprehensible!' In this closing chapter, it is not my intention to explain this doctrine. My main concern is to show how this specific doctrine casts light on the nature and purpose of doctrine in general. We begin by considering how the doctrine of the Trinity arises as a response to Christ.

THE TRINITY AND THE INCARNATION

In an earlier chapter (chapter 11), we considered the doctrine of the incarnation – the recognition that Jesus Christ is none other than God himself. We noted that this crucial insight can be justified on both the basis of the New Testament evidence and the Christian experience of God in the risen Christ. We also noted how the doctrine of the incarnation is essential to the fabric of the Christian faith. Remove or deny this insight, and the Christian faith, like a knitted garment, begins to unravel, lose its shape, and become of no significance. To abandon the idea of the incarnation is to end up with an understanding of Jesus as little more than an academic moralist, incapable of *understanding*, let alone *redeeming*, our situation. But for Christianity, God meets people precisely where they are – because he has already been there himself.

If Jesus *is* God, something very important about God himself is being implied. Is God to be identified with Jesus? How can we avoid suggesting that Jesus is a second God? After all, did not Jesus pray to God? And did not God remain in heaven during the earthly ministry of Jesus? In one sense, Jesus is God; in another, he isn't. Thus Jesus is God incarnate – but he still prays to God, without giving the slightest indication that he is talking to himself. Jesus is not *identical* with God, in that it is obvious that God continued to be in heaven during Jesus' lifetime – and yet Jesus may be *identified* with God, in that the New Testament has no hesitation in ascribing functions to Jesus which, properly speaking, only God could do. One way of dealing with the problem was to refer to God as 'Father', and Jesus as 'Son', or 'Son of God' (e.g., Rom. 1:3; 8:32; Heb. 4:14; 1 John 4:15) – thus indicating that they had the common bond of divinity, but that they could in some way be distinguished, with the Father being thought of as being in some way prior to the Son.

If Jesus Christ is God, the conclusion would seem to follow that God is to be identified totally with Jesus Christ. And yet it is obvious from Jesus' own teaching that he thought that God was still very much in heaven. The paradox we are beginning to wrestle with is expressed well by St Germanus, in his famous seventh century Christmas hymn:

> The Word becomes incarnate
> And yet remains on high!

The doctrine of the incarnation affirms that it really is God whom we encounter in Jesus Christ – but that this does not allow us to assert that Jesus and God are identical. It does not mean that God is *localised* in this one individual, Jesus Christ. Rather, it is stating that, because Jesus *is* God, he allows us to find out what God is like, to have a direct encounter with the reality of God. And because God is not totally identical with Jesus, he remains in heaven. God is just too big, too vast, for us to handle – and so God, knowing our weakness and accommodating himself to it (to use a helpful phrase due to John Calvin), makes himself available for us in a form which we can cope with. The doctrine of the incarnation affirms that it really is God whom we encounter directly in Jesus Christ – just as it affirms that God remains God throughout.

Recognising the divinity of Christ is one of the central pressures which leads to the doctrine of the Trinity. In asking questions like those just noted, we begin to travel down the path which leads to the distinctively Christian understanding of God – the doctrine of the Trinity. We have a long way to go before we arrive there – but by recognising that Jesus Christ is none other than God incarnate, we have set our feet firmly upon the road that leads to this most enigmatic of all Christian doctrines.

The relationship between the doctrines of the incarnation and the Trinity neatly illustrates a central theme of this book – the *coherence of Christian doctrine*. Individual Christian doctrines do not exist in non-interacting watertight compartments. They interact with, and modify, each other. They build up to give a coherent whole. Thus the recognition that Jesus is God immediately modifies any view of God which is incapable of coping with this insight. The history of the development of Christian doctrine shows this pattern clearly: once the full divinity of Jesus Christ was accepted as normative in the fourth century, the process of re-thinking the doctrine of God began in earnest. The culmination of this process is the doctrine of the Trinity.

Both historically and theologically, the doctrine of the Trinity can be shown to be a direct result of insights concerning the identity and significance of Jesus Christ. The doctrine of the Trinity is the end product of a long process of wrestling with two questions: 'Who and what must God be, if he was able to become incarnate in Jesus Christ? What must be true about God, if it is true that Jesus Christ is divine?' In coming to consider these questions, theologians were able to integrate certain key scriptural passages within this Christological context. In the following section, we shall examine these passages, with a view to demonstrating how doctrine integrates Scripture.

THE DOCTRINE OF THE TRINITY AND THE INTEGRATION OF SCRIPTURE

In one sense, there is no *doctrine* of the Trinity in the New Testament. Although the common work of the Father, Son and Holy Spirit is evident throughout the New Testament, there is no developed and comprehensive account of the precise manner in which these relate to one another. That this is the case should be the occasion for neither surprise nor disquiet. The New Testament is primarily concerned to witness to the *reality* of the Father, Son and Spirit; the doctrine of the Trinity is primarily reflection upon that reality by believers, as they attempt to make sense of it. The doctrine of the Trinity may not be present within the New Testament – but the saving revelation and action of God in Jesus Christ, which that doctrine attempts to interpret, is unquestionably at the heart of the New Testament proclamation.

Even within the New Testament itself, however, there are to be found clear hints of a trinitarian way of thinking. A number of key passages develop a triadic approach to God. The doctrine of the Trinity aims to integrate these passages, bringing out their common features and establishing their central insights concerning God. What sort of passages are we talking about? The most important are the following.

Matthew 28:19. 'Go and make disciples of all nations, baptising them in the name of the Father and of the Son and of the Holy Spirit'. Although baptism was initially performed in the name of Jesus (Acts 8:16; 19:5), this passage clearly indicates the implications of this practice. To be baptised in the name of Jesus is to be baptised in the name of the 'God and Father of our Lord Jesus' (1 Pet. 1:3).

2 Corinthians 13:14. 'May the grace of the Lord Jesus Christ, and the love of God, and the fellowship of the Holy Spirit be with you all.' This formula (which is echoed elsewhere in the New Testament – such as Rom. 16:20–21, 1 Cor. 16:23; 1 Thess. 5:28; 2 Thess. 3:18) is thought to be (or perhaps to echo) a very early Christian liturgical formula. This formula summarises the central aspects of the Christian understanding of God, clearly anticipating the later development of the formula into the doctrine of the Trinity.

2 Thessalonians 2:13–14. 'From the beginning God chose you to be saved through the sanctifying work of the Spirit and through belief in the truth. He called you to this through our gospel, that you might share in the glory of our Lord Jesus Christ.' This verse shows clearly how Paul's thought revolves around three sources of grace and salvation. Here, as elsewhere, Paul links these three sources together: grace and salvation derive from these three sources, which cannot be regarded as independent agencies. All three are involved in the same common work.

A series of such passages could be produced, all making the same fundamental point: salvation is the work of the Father, the Son and the Spirit. All three are involved, perhaps in different manners, in the process of salvation. The following texts are worth study in this respect: 1 Corinthians 12:4–6; 2 Corinthians 1:21–2; Galatians 4:6; Ephesians 2:20–22; 3:14–17; Titus 3:4–6; Hebrews 6:4; 1 Peter 1:2; Jude 20–21; Revelation 1:4–6. The doctrine of the Trinity aims to identify the central point being made by such passages, state it in a coherent and systematic form, and explore its implications.

THE DOCTRINE OF THE TRINITY IDENTIFIES THE CHRISTIAN GOD

One of the most important tasks facing early Christian writers was that of identifying the God they worshipped and adored. 'What God are you talking about?' was a frequent question put to them. A Jewish questioner would want to know how the 'God of the Christians' related to the 'God of Abraham, Isaac and Jacob'. Do Christians worship the same God as the Jews – or someone else?

As Christianity expanded into the Mediterranean world of the second century, it began to encounter religious rivals, which again forced Christian theologians to identify their God, and distinguish him from potential alternatives. A powerful threat to Christianity was posed by Gnosticism in the second century. Gnosticism, as we have seen, represented a complicated and diverse bundle of beliefs, many very similar to those of the Christian church. For example, it laid great stress on the importance of personal salvation. But it also differed from Christianity at a number of crucial points, including the notion of God. Gnosticism argued that there were *two* gods. The first was responsible for the creation of the world; the second was responsible for its redemption. Most Gnostics treated the creator god as a second-rate deity, and gave priority to the redeemer god.

This alarmed Christian theologians, who saw a real danger in these beliefs. For example, they might suggest that the god of the Old Testament was simply responsible for creating the world, while the god of the New Testament was responsible for the much more important and prestigious work of redemption. To confuse the Christian and Gnostic gods could lead to a serious perversion of the gospel. Accordingly, Christian theologians – such as the second-century writer Irenaeus of Lyons – insisted that the God of the Old and New Testaments was one and the same. It was one and the same God who created the world, who redeemed it through Jesus Christ, and who is now present through his Spirit. As Robert Jenson has stressed in his *Triune Identity*, the doctrine of the Trinity thus served to distinguish Christianity from its rivals, by identifying the God whom Christians knew, worshipped and adored.

The Trinity thus came to be seen almost as something approaching a proper name. There are obvious parallels between the Christian phrase 'Father, Son and Holy Spirit' (Matt. 28:19; 2 Cor. 13:14) and its Old Testament predecessor 'the God of Abraham, Isaac and Jacob'. Both *identify* the God in question. Question: what God are you talking about? Answer: the God who raised Jesus Christ from the dead, and is now present through the Spirit. The trinitarian formula is a shorthand way of identifying exactly what God we are talking about. Christianity packs into this one neat phrase the high points of the history of God's redeeming work, the big moments (resurrection and Pentecost) when God was so clearly present and active. It specifically links God with these events, just as Israel specifically linked God with the Exodus from Egypt. It focuses our attention on events, events in which God's presence and activity were to be found concentrated and publicly demonstrated.

The doctrine of the Trinity thus identifies the God of Christianity, and clarifies his relation to potential rivals. (Thus, to give but one example, the 'God and Father of our Lord Jesus Christ' is the same as the 'God of Abraham, Isaac and Jacob', but is to be distinguished from Gnostic concepts of God.) And by identifying God in this way, the doctrine of the Trinity also identifies the Christian church. It marks it off from religious rivals – such as unitarianism (the denial of the divinity of Christ and the Holy Spirit) – which might otherwise seem very similar to Christianity.

THE DOCTRINE OF THE TRINITY INTERPRETS
THE SCRIPTURAL NARRATIVE

Scripture tells the story of God's dealings with humanity, reaching its climax in the history of Jesus Christ. The story neither begins nor ends with the coming of Christ; nevertheless, his coming divides that story in two. For Christians, Christ is the centre of time. Yet God was active before the coming of Christ, and remains active afterwards. Scripture tells the story of the actions of God in history.

Yet that story is complex. God acts in different ways at different points. One of the central themes of the New Testament is that it tells the story of the same God as the Old Testament. The 'God of Abraham, Isaac and Jacob' is the same as the 'God and Father of our Lord Jesus Christ'. The doctrine of the Trinity gives us a framework for making sense of the acts of God in history, as they are told in the scriptural narrative. How is the Exodus from Egypt related to the resurrection of Jesus Christ? Or to the coming of the Holy Spirit at Pentecost? The doctrine of the Trinity interprets the great scriptural story, making it clear that it is one and the same God who is present and active throughout the story of our redemption.

Tertullian, the third-century Christian writer, gave us a particularly helpful way of beginning to make sense of the scriptural narrative. He suggested that we think of 'one God in three persons'. For Tertullian, the word 'person' seems to have meant 'a role in a drama'. (The Latin word *persona* originally meant 'mask', and by a process of transference, came to mean 'the role played in a theatre'. Roman actors wore masks to represent the different characters which they played.) The phrase 'one God in three persons' could be interpreted along the following lines. In the great drama of human redemption, three different roles are played out. These are the roles of the creator, the redeemer and the sanctifier. All these three roles are played by the same actor – God. The roles of Father, Son and Spirit are not played by three independent actors. 'Three persons but one God' means 'three roles, but one actor'. Behind the richness of the scriptural account of redemption is to be discerned the action of one and the same God.

THE DOCTRINE OF THE TRINITY INTERPRETS CHRISTIAN EXPERIENCE

As we stressed earlier, one of the classic functions of Christian doctrine is to interpret Christian experience. For example, we noted how the doctrines of the fall and redemption gave new meaning to the deep sense of 'longing' within human nature, which proves incapable of being satisfied by any finite object (pp. 44–9). The doctrine of the Trinity brings new meaning and depth to the whole area of Christian experience, especially in the specific areas of worship and prayer.

Christians pray to God almost as a matter of instinct – it seems to come to them naturally. As they kneel down to say their prayers, they are aware that in some way (which is very difficult to express in words) God is actually *prompting* them to pray. It is almost as if God is at work within them, creating a desire to pray, or to turn to God in worship and adoration. Yet God is also the one to whom they are praying. A similar situation arises in worship. Although it is God whom we are praising, we are aware that it is somehow God himself who moves us from within to praise him. And theologians have captured this mystery in the formula 'to the Father, through the Son and in the Holy Spirit'. In prayer and worship alike, we seem to be brought before the presence of the Father, through the mediation of the Son, in the power of the Holy Spirit.

And that, in conclusion, is the function of doctrine itself – to bring us and others safely into the presence of God, and hold us there.

CONCLUSION

The present work has aimed to examine and explain the purpose and place of Christian doctrine. It is responsible and obedient reflection on the part of the church on the mysteries of faith. Doctrine preserves the Christian church from woolly and confused understandings of its identity and calling, and provides believers with a framework for interpreting the ambiguities of human experience. It is the natural outcome of Christian reflection on the mysteries of faith. It allows the ambiguities of human experience in the world to be interpreted and transformed. It opens the way to the construction of a world-view, through which Christian attitudes and approaches to a range of matters – social, spiritual, ethical and political – can be developed.

The idea of 'Christianity without doctrine' will doubtless continue to tantalise those who, for one reason or another, find doctrine pedantic, petty, or pointless. The present work is written in the conviction that doctrine, rightly understood, is nothing of the sort. Inadequate, weak and unsympathetic accounts of the nature of doctrine may indeed create this impression. Doctrine may at times seem to be something of an irrelevance – but on closer inspection it holds the key to the future of the Christian faith in the modern world. The church cannot think, let alone act, without basing its thoughts and actions upon a doctrinal foundation. Doctrine must continue to be, and to be *allowed and recognised to be*, a central resource in Christian education. Christianity is irreducibly doctrinal in its foundations, upon which a considerable experiential, social and political superstructure may be erected. The foundation must be capable of supporting this structure. To neglect – still worse, to repudiate – this foundation is to deny the Christian church the critical resources it needs if it is to retain its identity and mission in the third millennium of its existence.

Bibliography

The list of books and articles below is intended to allow the reader to develop at least some of the ideas found in this work to whatever level seems appropriate. A common difficulty encountered by many readers concerns the level at which works are written. Some of the more severely academic works are written with the needs of specialists in mind, and make no allowance for the general reader. Those marked with an asterisk (*) are especially suitable as introductory texts, and are generally easier to read than the present work. Those marked with a dagger (†) are somewhat technical, and may prove considerably more difficult to read than this book. The extra effort required, however, should be found to be merited.

This bibliography includes all those works cited in the text itself.

Atkinson, James, and Williams, Rowan, 'On Doing Theology', in C. Baxter (ed.), *Stepping Stones* (London: Hodder & Stoughton, 1987), 1–20.

Avis, Paul, *Ecumenical Theology and the Elusiveness of Doctrine* (London: SPCK, 1986).

Barth, Karl, *Evangelical Theology: An Introduction* (London: Weidenfeld & Nicolson, 1968).

Bauckham, Richard, 'The Worship of Jesus in Apocalyptic Christianity', *New Testament Studies* 27 (1980), 322–41.

— and Williams, Rowan, 'Jesus – God with Us', in C. Baxter

(ed.), *Stepping Stones* (London: Hodder & Stoughton, 1987), 21–41.

Berkhof, Hendrikus, *Christian Faith: An Introduction to the Study of the Faith* (Grand Rapids: Eerdmans, 1980).

Boff, Leonardo, *Trinity and Society* (London: Burns & Oates, 1988).

Brown, David, *The Divine Trinity* (London: Duckworth, 1985).

Brown, Harold O. J., *Heresies: The Image of Christ in the Mirror of Heresy and Orthodoxy* (Garden City, N.Y.: Doubleday, 1984).

Carson, D. A., and Woodbridge, John D. (eds.), *Scripture and Truth* (Leicester: Inter-Varsity Press, 1983).

†Christian, W. A., *Doctrines of Religious Communities: A Philosophical Study* (New Haven: Yale University Press, 1987).

Curran, Charles E., *Themes in Fundamental Moral Theology* (Notre Dame: University of Notre Dame Press, 1977).

†Dunn, J. D. G., *Christology in the Making* (London: SCM Press, 1989).

Forsyth, P. T., *The Person and Place of Jesus Christ* (London: Independent Press, 1909).

France, R. T., 'The Worship of Jesus: A Neglected Factor in Christological Debate?', in H. H. Rowdon (ed.), *Christ The Lord* (Leicester: Inter-Varsity Press, 1982), 17–36.

Gore, Charles, *The Incarnation of the Son of God* (London: John Murray, 1922).

†Jenson, Robert, *The Triune Identity: God According to the Gospel* (Philadelphia: Fortress Press, 1982).

Kelly, J. N. D., *Early Christian Creeds* (London: Longmans, 3rd edn, 1982).

†Lash, Nicholas, *Easter in Ordinary: Reflections on Human Experience and the Knowledge of God* (London: SCM Press, 1988).

Lewis, C. S., *Surprised by Joy* (London: Collins, 1955).

—, *Till We Have Faces* (London: Collins, 1956).

—, 'The Weight of Glory', in *Screwtape Proposes a Toast* (London: Collins, 1965), 94–110.

—, 'The Language of Religion', in *Christian Reflections* (London: Collins, 1981), 164–79.

†Lindbeck, George, *The Nature of Doctrine* (Philadelphia: Fortress Press, 1984).

†McGrath, Alister E., *The Making of Modern German Christology* (Oxford: Basil Blackwell, 1986).

*—, *Understanding Jesus: Who Jesus Christ is and why he matters* (Eastbourne: Kingsway Publications, 1989).

*—, *Understanding the Trinity* (Eastbourne: Kingsway Publications, 1990).

†—, *The Genesis of Doctrine: A Study in the Foundations of Doctrinal Criticism* (Oxford/Cambridge, Mass.: Blackwells, 1990).

*—, *The Basics of Faith: A Study Guide to the Apostles' Creed* (Leicester: Inter-Varsity Press, 1991).

†MacIntyre, Alasdair, *Whose Justice? Which Rationality?* (Notre Dame: University of Notre Dame, 1988).

†Mahoney, John, *The Making of Moral Theology* (Oxford University Press, 1989).

Marshall, I. Howard, *The Origins of New Testament Christology* (Leicester: Inter-Varsity Press, 1976).

—, 'Incarnational Christology in the New Testament', in H. H. Rowdon (ed.), *Christ the Lord* (Leicester: Inter-Varsity Press, 1982), 1–16.

Mitchell, Basil, 'Is there a distinctive Christian ethic?', in *How to Play Theological Ping-Pong* (London: Hodder & Stoughton, 1990), 42–56.

Moule, C. F. D., *The Origin of Christology* (Cambridge: Cambridge University Press, 1978).

†O'Donovan, Oliver, *Resurrection and Moral Order* (Leicester: Inter-Varsity Press, 1986).

Reid, J. K. S., *The Authority of Scripture* (London: Greenwood Press, 1981).

Sayers, Dorothy L., 'Creed or Chaos?', in *Creed or Chaos?* (London: Methuen, 1947), pp. 25–46.

Stott, J. R. W., *The Cross of Christ* (Leicester: Inter-Varsity Press, 1989).

†Stout, Jeffrey, *Ethics after Babel* (Cambridge: James Clarke, 1990).

Taylor, A. E., *The Faith of a Moralist* (2 vols: London: Macmillan, 1930).

Thielicke, Helmut, *Theological Ethics* (3 vols: Grand Rapids: Eerdmans, 1978).

Torrance, T. F., *The Trinitarian Faith* (Edinburgh: T & T Clark, 1988).

†Williams, Rowan, *Arius: Heresy and Tradition* (London: Darton, Longman & Todd, 1987).

—, 'The Incarnation as the Basis of Dogma', in R. Morgan (ed.), *The Religion of the Incarnation* (Bristol: Bristol Classical Press, 1989), 85–98.